The Treasure House of Early American Rooms

The Treasure House of

EARLY AMERICAN ROOMS

JOHN A. H. SWEENEY

Photographs by Gilbert Ask

INTRODUCTION BY HENRY FRANCIS DU PONT

A Winterthur Book

W · W · NORTON & COMPANY
New York   London

Library of Congress Catalog Card Number: 63-15585

0-393-01601-3 CLOTHBOUND
0-393-30039-0 PAPERBOUND

W. W. Norton & Company, Inc. 500 Fifth Avenue, New York, NY 10110
W. W. Norton & Company Ltd. 37 Great Russell Street, London WC1B 3NU

1 2 3 4 5 6 7 8 9 0

Contents

The Building of Winterthur Museum

by Henry Francis du Pont

Winterthur, in Christiana Hundred, New Castle County, Delaware, was so called by its first owner, James Antoine Bidermann, son of an eminent Paris banker. He was born in 1790 and came to the United States in 1814 with letters of introduction from the Marquis de Lafayette to friends in America. He made a trip through the West—possibly as far as the Mississippi—and after that came back to Delaware.

On September 14, 1816, he was married to Evelina Gabrielle, daughter of Eleuthère Irénée du Pont de Nemours, and granddaughter of Pierre Samuel du Pont de Nemours, French economist and political writer, who emigrated with his family to America in the autumn of 1799.

In 1837 James Antoine Bidermann purchased from the estate of his father-in-law four tracts of land in Christiana Hundred comprised of several hundred acres, of which part had been known as the Martin and Clenny farms. Upon the Clenny land he built a house which was named *Winterthur* for the Swiss city from which the Bidermann ancestors had come. It was of brick and stucco, with a flat roof, a porte-cochere at the front, and a porch at the back; and the Bidermann family moved into this new house in 1839.

Upon the death of his father, June 8, 1865, James Irénée Bidermann, who was living in France, became the owner of Winterthur. In February, 1867, he and his wife sold the estate, consisting of some 445 acres, to his uncle, Henry du Pont, who later added to his holdings by the purchase of adjoining farms.

My father, Henry A. du Pont, the son of Henry, after he moved to Winterthur in 1876, replaced the flat roof with a steep slate roof and dormer windows and added tall brick chimneys. When he inherited the property in 1889, he further enlarged the estate, building many roads and paths, enlarging the lawns around the house, and planting numerous trees and shrubs.

In 1902 my father added a new front, one room deep, as well as the wing including the Billiard Room, Library, and Squash Court. The Billiard Room is now the Morattico Hall and Flock Room; and the Squash Court includes the Oyster Bay Room and Hart Room, on the lower level, and the Queen Anne Dining Room and Pennsylvania Folk Art Room, on the upper level. The slate roof was replaced by heavy Spanish tiles, and the old wooden cornices and the dormers were replaced by terra-cotta cornices and by Francis I dormers.

At the death of my father, on the thirty-first of December, 1926, I took over the estate.

After the beginning of the First World War, my father was in England for many weeks and saw with me many beautiful and interesting English places. On his return he planted many conifers on a sloping hillside and below them we put two *en tout cas* tennis courts. Some years after his death I laid out paths among the conifers, planted the Chaenomeles Walk, and in 1956 I took out the tennis courts and planned a semiformal garden there with eight very large Chaenomeles. My lifelong friend Miss Marian Cruger Coffin, the landscape architect, designed the four beds planted with *Lonicera nitida* around the armillary sundial I had moved there from our garden at the swimming pool, two terraces of which had to make way for a visitors' parking area.

I enlarged the house in 1929. The elaborate Spanish tiles were removed and a simple terra-cotta tile roof put on, and the new dormers and cornices of cast stone were made reproducing those on the Port Royal house at Frankford, Pennsylvania. The original dormers from which they were copied are on the roof of the small wing in which are the rug, curtain, and bedspread rooms. The porte-cochere on the north side of the house was removed and in its place was put a glass-enclosed conservatory, and a new entrance was made on the west side. The entrance door here is the original one from Port Royal, and the façade a copy from Port Royal. The Dining Room Porch columns were copied from the Woodlands, built in 1788 and still standing in West Philadelphia; the Conservatory pilasters were copied from another side of the same house.

Several years before the addition of the new wing in 1929, I had bought all the quoins, stone window sills, Palladian windows, and interior woodwork from Port Royal, built in 1762 in Frankford, Pennsylvania. The latter was put in the Entrance Hall (p. 63) and Port Royal Parlor (p. 65), in the Port Royal Bedroom and the Maple Room. The Chestertown Room (p. 54) came from a house at 107 Water Street in Chestertown, Maryland, built about 1762, and the plaster decoration is from a ceiling in Port Royal. The woodwork from Belle Isle, built by William Bertrand before 1760 at Litwalton, Lancaster County, Virginia, I put in the Belle Isle and Walnut Rooms (p. 29), and also in the Lancaster Room, and in the stairs which go to the Oyster Bay Room (p. 22) and Hart Room (p. 20). The woodwork and stairs from Readbourne, built in Queen Anne's County, Maryland, about 1733, were put in the Readbourne Parlor (p. 44) and Stair Hall (p. 46), the stairs going from the entrance to the floor above, and also in the New York Bedroom and the Du Pont Dining Room (p. 108). The Essex Room came from the Ritchie house, built at Tappahannock, Virginia, before 1725. The Hampton Room came from Hampton Court, built in Elizabeth, New Jersey, 1761, and the Cecil Bedroom (p. 34) came from a house built about 1730 near Northeast, Cecil County, Maryland. Some Philadelphia woodwork and mantels with scenes of the Battle of Lake Erie were installed in the McIntire Bedroom (p. 88), Lake Erie Hall, and Baltimore Drawing Room (p. 124). In the Imlay Room (p. 120), from Allentown, New Jersey, are the wallpaper and original Venetian blinds. This house was built about 1790. There is also a Philadelphia mantel with the heads of Washington and Franklin from the Peter Breen house, 249 South Tenth Street.

Across the hall is the Albany Room, so named because it had always had a four-post bed belonging to my great-uncle Jacob Ten Eyck, of Albany. It was hung with pink-and-white bird chintz, now used part of the year in the Franklin Room. In the Albany Room, I put a Philadelphia mantel with a very tall, narrow opening.

The new wing was completed in the spring of 1931; and when we moved in, we were much pleased with our new period rooms and with the Chinese Parlor (p. 68), which formerly had been the dining room, sitting room, and hall of the 1839 house, and which made a good transition between the old and the new house. Directly under this room was the Pine Kitchen, which was also put in during 1929 in the space which was formerly the 1839 kitchen. In the adjacent laundry, I put the Wentworth Room from the Samuel Wentworth house, built in the seventeenth century in Portsmouth, New Hampshire, with paneling dating probably about 1710. Above it, next to the Chinese Parlor, is the Empire Parlor (p. 128), formerly the 1839 living room and my father's office. In the 1902 changes, these two rooms were made into a Louis XVI room. The elevator hall, on this floor, was originally our main entrance hall and where the elevator is was the only staircase in the house, a built-in spiral stairs lighted by a skylight in the third floor ceiling.

In 1933 my great friend Mrs. Harry Horton Benkard told me about the house at Patuxent Manor at Lower Marlboro, Maryland, built about 1744; and I was lucky enough to obtain the woodwork of the hall and the two entrance floor rooms, which were identical in height and paneling. I say "lucky" because that paneling fitted exactly into the Marlboro Room (p. 74), even to the size of the windows; so in 1934 I took out the Italian ceiling and the red damask off the walls, and installed the Marlboro woodwork and gave the room its new name. At the same time, the remainder of the woodwork of the Patuxent Manor house was installed in the bedroom directly above it, and that room was called the Patuxent Room (p. 72). That same year I also put the mantelpiece with the heads of Lafayette and Washington in the Blue Room (p. 115), and two old doorways and trim from the Wilson house in Salem, New Jersey, built between 1805 and 1810.

When we went on a world tour in 1936, I took out the marble staircase with bronze railing which had been added to the house in 1902, and replaced it with the spiral staircase from Montmorenci, a house built about 1822 near Shocco

Springs, Warren County, North Carolina, also using there all the doors, door trim, and beautiful triple windows and plaster cornices. I used the woodwork from that same house in the Library Hall and Cross Hall (p. 80), keeping the original color, and did the same in the Nemours Room (p. 110). In 1936 I also installed the Bulfinch staircase from a house designed by Charles Bulfinch in 1795 at Bowdoin and Cambridge Streets, Boston, which my architect, Thomas T. Waterman, had salvaged when he was working with Cram and Ferguson, of Boston, from 1920 to 1926. The stairs lead to the Bulfinch Stair Hall, where I used the archway from the Ezekiel Hersey Derby house in Salem, Massachusetts, about 1800, possibly carved by Samuel McIntire.

In 1937 I sheathed two sides of a large closet opening into the elevator hall, near the Pine Kitchen, with plain boards, and in the three shallow closets there installed my collection of Pennsylvania hinges, latches, etc. At the end of the room, standing on a sill with a curved blue-and-white sky-painted background, is a 1670 New York weather vane and also large-sized 1637 iron numerals on the side of the background.

To my delight, in 1938 I was able to do away with the Squash Tennis Court, as the great majority of our friends would play only squash racquets, which required a much larger court. At the east end of the court, I put the bedroom of the 1670 Thomas Hart house from Ipswich, Massachusetts, which I had obtained from the Metropolitan Museum, and the little staircase from the Belle Isle house was used to get down to it. Directly above the Hart Room (p. 20), I installed the Queen Anne Dining Room (p. 41) with woodwork from New Hampshire, thus getting two stories of rooms in the Squash Court. This beautiful blue-green room had been covered with hideous modern paint which my painter, Park McCann, removed with painstaking patience and skill. Next to the Queen Anne Dining Room is the Pennsylvania Folk Art Room (p. 170), without cornices and with deep, curved window jambs as in nearby Pennsylvania rooms of that period. In this room, a pair of superb Pennsylvania church doors, with the original hardware, opened into a little Connecticut glass room.

Next to the Belle Isle Hall and the Salem Stair Hall, I put in the Vauxhall Room (p. 43) from Cumberland County, New Jersey, with flock paper which also has an unusual dado, and on the floor directly above it, the Phyfe Room (p. 112), with the woodwork and mahogany doors from the Moses Rogers house at 7 State Street, facing the Battery, in New York; next to the Phyfe Room, the Phyfe Vestibule, with doors and overdoors from a downtown New York house; and next to that, the Salem Stair Hall (p. 82) with fine newel posts from Salem, Massachusetts; and beyond that, the Eagle Room, whose built-in glazed cupboards house a Chinese export porcelain service decorated with the American eagle and a brown-and-tan border, which belonged to Princess George Chavchavadze, whose grandmothers were a Miss Willing, of Philadelphia, and a Miss Monroe, of New York; or possibly it might have belonged to the mother of her first husband, Comte Jacques de Breteuil, who was a Miss Phillips, of Philadelphia.

In 1938 I also put some charming woodwork from Georgetown, District of Columbia, in the China Hall (p. 79), which connects with the Chinese Parlor, the Baltimore Room, and the Dining Room Hall, and has, in two of its four niches, the Cincinnati dinner service which belonged to George Washington.

In 1939 Mrs. Frank McFadden asked me to come and see some of her furniture which she wished to sell; I did so and was struck with the superb fireplace wall, cornice, and doorways of her dining room, which, by the way, was entirely paneled and had a large bay window almost as large as the room. I was much interested to hear it had come from the Blackwell house on Pine Street in Philadelphia, built about 1764; and I am glad to say she very kindly sold the woodwork to me and also the mantel from the adjoining room, now in the Chinese Parlor. The Philadelphia Museum, in one of its bulletins, had written up the room in detail; and when I removed the woodwork, I gave her an old mantel and a simple cornice and left, of course, the paneled walls which did not belong to the room. It took a year to relocate the windows and all the heating pipes going to the floor above and to tear out closets and so forth, before I installed the room which is now called the Blackwell Parlor (p. 66). Without changing it in the slightest degree, it just fitted in the narrowest space there was in the house. Fortunately, the vestibule, with a mahogany dado and doorway from the Blackwell house hall, opened into the Port Royal Parlor and connected the two rooms.

In 1940 most of my activities were on the eighth floor, and I built an outside elevator to bring up the beams and paneling of the Hardenbergh Parlor and Bedroom (pp. 37 to 39), which came from the Hardenbergh house, Ulster County, New York, built in 1762. Both of these beamed-ceiling rooms have paneled fireplace walls, which is fairly unusual. The date of the house and the owner's name are carved on a stone above the entrance to the bedroom. Next to the Hardenbergh Bedroom is the Spatterware Hall (p. 173) with the staircase from the Wright house, Wethersfield, Connecticut, 1784, going to the Scrimshaw Room above. On one side is the Spatterware Vestibule, with a door from the Cornelius du Puy house, built about 1690 at Accord, New York, opening into the Stoneware Closet; and at the other side is the door to the Simsbury, Connecticut, Room (p. 58) with its boxed, or paneled, summer beam, the only one at Winterthur. Beyond that is the little William and Mary Room. On the north side of the Hardenbergh Bedroom is the Lebanon Room, from Lebanon, Pennsylvania, with strap hinges on the door, and beyond that, the Lebanon Bedroom (p. 178). The Dresser Room (p. 176) is on the other side of the Lebanon Room, so called because of its four Pennsylvania dressers. To the east, beyond the Bulfinch Stair Hall, is the Pennsylvania German Bedroom (p. 175), with its framed plaster overmantel from a house near Lancaster, Pennsylvania, about 1780, decorated with three urns, and from the center one, an important spray with birds in the foliage; then the Pennsylvania German Child's Bedroom, and the Chippendale Stair Hall, with its stair from a house near Franklin, Virginia. Opening from the Chippendale Stair Hall is the Child's Room with one of the few child's high-post beds, and the Glass Alcove and five shelves with many glass oil lamps lighted.

In 1940 in the Sheraton Room (p. 90), I eliminated the closet and installed the 1785 woodwork from Mordington, near Frederica, Delaware; and installed, two floors below, the woodwork in the Flock Room (p. 27) and Morattico Hall (p. 25) from Morattico, Richmond County, Virginia.

The Flock Room, about 1715, is one of the very few large-sized rooms of that period. It has a high dado and most interesting marbleized and painted wood panels on the fireplace wall. These panels my friend Charles MacLellan, the artist, got for me in Virginia in 1929; and had it not been for the painstaking work and knowledge of my architect, Thomas T. Waterman, the woodwork of the same room which I got much later could never have been assembled. On the walls above the dado there is a flock covering in a rich patern of green, orange, and gray.

Also in 1940 I did away with the Louis XVI room next to the Chinese Parlor. I took out the pilasters and the Louis XVI woodwork and made it into the Empire Parlor (p. 128). The woodwork and cherry doors came from the house of Rufus King, 2 Elk Street, Albany, New York; and the Italian marble mantelpiece, with its two figures in relief, came from a downtown New York house where such mantels were used at that period.

In 1941, by reducing the length of the Essex Room closet, I installed in the hall a china alcove with woodwork from Montmorenci. The handsome fanlight above the shelves gives into the Essex Hall and also gets light from the window there. To the east of the Imlay Room, after removing two-thirds of a bathroom, I made the Portsmouth Room (p. 92) by putting in the windows and simple woodwork from an early nineteenth-century house in Portsmouth, New Hampshire. These windows have the characteristic Portsmouth sliding two-part wood shutters.

On the floor directly under this room, by reducing the bathroom precisely as the one above and using some old Philadelphia woodwork, I made the Empire Bedroom (p. 132). This connects with the McIntire Bedroom (p. 88) which has Philadelphia woodwork intricately modeled in stucco and painted dove gray. The composition ornament on the doorframes, the mantel with the Battle of Lake Erie, and cornice was probably done, like that in the Baltimore Drawing Room, by Robert Wellford. In the hall between the McIntire Bedroom and the Franklin Room I put the Lake Erie mantel, signed by Wellford and with the inscription *We Have Met the Enemy and They Are Ours,* and woodwork from Montmorenci. The Franklin Room (p. 96) is one of the original bedrooms in the 1839 house; and here I put the marble mantel from the Edward Everett house, 16 Harvard Street, Charlestown, Massachusetts—the only marble mantel, to my knowledge, with the head of Franklin on it. The door and wainscoting came from an eighteenth-century Baltimore house. In this room the fabric of the bed and window curtains is the famous copperplate-printed cotton called the *Apotheosis of Franklin;* its design includes a full-length portrait of Franklin acclaimed by Liberty, Columbia, and Fame.

Next to the Franklin Room I put in some old Philadelphia woodwork. This room is called the Gold and White Room (p. 107) because of the white-and-gold bed, settee, and chairs formerly belonging to Governor Yates of New York, the white-and-gold Salem dressing table, and a presentation timepiece by Simon Willard.

Also in 1941, by removing the Patuxent Room closets and including them and the Philadelphia room closet with the Philadelphia Bedroom (p. 70), this room became a good-sized room with green-and-brown dado and doorways from Chestertown, Maryland. Owing to the Conservatory roof, the lower part of the window has to have a sash curtain which I copied from an engraving, a photograph of which is in a drawer in the room. I also put in this room some eighteenth-century Chinese paper. This room opens into the Philadelphia Hall, where I put the Chippendale doorway and cornice from the house in Philadelphia occupied in 1761 by Solomon Engels, and a very interesting silk-embroidered wall covering found in a chateau in Southern France.

In 1942 I heard that Miss Mary Latimer's charming yellow stucco house, "Latimeria," on the south side of Wilmington was about to be torn down. Leslie Potts, who has helped in all the changes in the house and Museum, went over there and was able to get the shelves for a little room which I called the Latimeria Room. This was formerly a big closet beside the Port Royal Parlor in which I succeeded in putting a small window. I was particularly interested in the Latimer house as the original owner, William Warner, had come to my great-grandfather Irénée du Pont and asked him to draw plans for a house. My great-grandfather marked three sheets of paper: *Good, Better, Best.* Mr. Warner chose the one marked *Good.* The one marked *Better* was a simpler house, and the one marked *Best* was a blank piece of paper. Some time after the house was built the gentleman failed, and the Latimers bought it. After Miss Latimer's death I bought from her estate the lattice summerhouse which is in the Saunders peony garden, and also the pair of wood beehives on each side of the wide steps, and the Chinese pagoda doorway at the end of the Azalea "magnifica" garden beyond the Saunders peonies.

In 1945 I made the Baltimore Room (p. 122) by enclosing the porch which gave on the Empire Parlor and China Hall and used there one of the triple windows from Montmorenci, and its dado, and placed above it part of the Bay of Naples wallpaper.

In 1946 at the north end of the sixth floor I took out the two bathrooms and made the Empire Hall (p. 130) with the two north windows giving light as far as the elevator and Lake Erie Hall. The woodwork comes from Montmorenci. Also on this floor I made the Powel Room by taking out the Walnut room and hall closets and combining the space with the Walnut bathroom. In this room is an original cornice from one of the rooms of the Powel house in Philadelphia.

Until 1947 the room beside the Hart Room was for furniture display. That year I put there the beamed ceiling and woodwork from the Job Wright house in Oyster Bay, Long Island, and called it the Oyster Bay Room (p. 22), and used the fireplace lintel from a contemporary house in Milford, Connecticut, with carved ornament consisting of a single row of diamond-shaped points. In the little room beside it I put in the wood ceiling and woodwork of a log house on the Mount Pleasant Road in St. Georges Hundred, in New Castle County, Delaware, and then named it the Delaware Room.

Realizing the house was soon to be a museum, in 1947 to 1948 I installed in the Badminton Court, with some modifications, the façades of four houses, three of which have several rooms and staircases in the Museum, and put in during these two years the Blue Staffordshire Room; the Commons Room (p. 119); the Counting Room (p. 101) and stairs; End Shop (p. 156) and stairs; Shop Lane (p. 152) with its six shop fronts; China Shop (p. 140), opening into Tappahannock

Hall (p. 33); the Tappahannock Room (p. 31); Bertrand Room (p. 61), Hall, and Vestibule. I also built the wing with its curtain, carpet, and bedspread rooms, and carpenter and paint shops on the ground floor; also the Schimmel Hall, leading to the Court, and the visitors' dining room and sitting room. There was enough old trim to put a window in the closet beside the Du Pont Dining Room; and I put the shelves there from a little country store at Chelsea, Delaware County, Pennsylvania, which I watched for many years and then almost lost. This room is the Candlestick Room.

In 1949 I put in the Glass Room on the top floor, with a large collection of Amelung, Stiegel-type, South Jersey, and other American glass, which has the benefit of sunlight as well as artificial light, using there also the charming curved dado from the country store at Chelsea, Pennsylvania.

After we left the house in January, 1951, many bathrooms were taken out and in their place were put the Cecil Sitting Room, Music Room, the Essex Hall, the Architect's Room (p. 95) with mantel from an old house in Connecticut and a three-part window; and the New York Bedroom was made larger. The Blue Dressing Room closets provided space for the Winterthur Bedroom (p. 91). It has the woodwork of the house as it was first built. The Maple Hall and Massachusetts Hall were installed. Built at this time was the Visitors' Entrance which connected with Schimmel Hall.

During 1952, at the west end of the house, the false ceiling in the old wine cellar under the Marlboro Room was taken out and the pipes changed. The soil on the outside was taken away and two windows put in, and then the Fraktur Room, from the David Hottenstein house near Kutztown, Berks County, Pennsylvania, was installed. There is a door on the south side of the room near the corner cupboard and windows each side of the mantel on the north side and one window on the east side. This room, with its painted and spattered wainscot and woodwork, has its exact original proportions. The new east doorway opens into the Frederica Hall, with its painted red-and-blue carved eagle from the Willow Brook house, Kernstown, Virginia, about 1800. The Dunlap Room, which was also installed in 1952, from Bedford, New Hampshire, has its one door opening into the Frederica Hall. The woodwork in this room has its original

paint, and the carved motives of the cornice are the same as on the maple high chest and desk by Samuel Dunlap. In 1963 we are fortunate enough to widen it to the original size.

In 1953 what I thought to be the last new period room in the Museum was made by including in one room the Belle Isle bath, hall, and closets. The woodwork is painted blue, and the room is called the Wynkoop Room because of this color, which is the same blue as that in one of the rooms in the Wynkoop house at Stone Ridge, Ulster County, New York. The room was made for the first Spanish-foot bed I ever had the opportunity to buy. All the other pieces of furniture in the room have Spanish feet also. I considered this to be a fitting climax to the completion of the Museum, but in 1957 Mr. Sommer found the Kershner house in the country near Reading, Pennsylvania. It had an extraordinary plaster ceiling in the main room and a huge fireplace in the kitchen. These two rooms we put in place of the Pine Kitchen at Winterthur, and to do so we had to push the wall of the room out about twelve inches.

When the Museum determined to build the new wing, which is now called the South Wing, it was decided to include a group of rooms that could be seen by people any time they wished to come and also for school children to see. These rooms are all from New England except the Queen Anne Bedroom, which comes from a house on Cuthbert Street in Philadelphia, and a marvelous painted stair hall from East Springfield, New York, which is near Cooperstown. The Empire Hall has trim from the original part of the house here at Winterthur.

The dining room for visitors had proved to be rather small, and in the new wing was included a large new dining room with woodwork from the Burrows house at Charleston, South Carolina. It had been acquired a number of years ago by Francis P. Garvan, who gave it to Yale University. They never used it and so were glad to let us have it. Outside the bay window I arranged a space for a small garden. The sitting room for the visitors has paneling from the Bowers house at Somerset, Massachusetts, which was built in the 1760's, and so has the adjoining Somerset Room.

When the South Wing was completed, we put our minds to using some woodwork which had been here for quite a

The Memorial Library is a second-floor room in the wing added in 1902 by Henry Algernon du Pont, whose portrait, painted in 1906 by Ellen Emmett, hangs above the fireplace. Over the sofa is a portrait of Henry Francis du Pont by the same artist, and a recent one by Andrew Wyeth hangs between the windows. Books owned by Henry A. du Pont fill the shelves. The Chippendale chairs are upholstered with leather from the Winterthur herd. In the center of the room a scale model of the house indicates its size and plan and the changes made to it by four owners through the years.

while; and on the top floor, where there had been a studio for the photographer, Robert Raley designed an installation for the woodwork which came from the Shaker village at Enfield, New Hampshire. This woodwork has its original yellow paint, and it forms two rooms which provide a place for a number of pieces of Shaker furniture which had been given to the Museum some years ago. Next to the Shaker rooms we installed a large room for the display of pottery and used in it the wonderful Pennsylvania German church doors which had been in the Pennsylvania Folk Art Room. This work was begun in 1960, but it took nearly two years to finish.

While this was being done we had made a little room called the Vickers Alcove out of a bathroom near the Montmorenci Stair Hall and installed a collection of porcelain plates made by John Vickers, of Chester County, Pennsylvania, in 1824, a year before the porcelain made by Tucker in Philadelphia. Also we moved back the wall at the top of the Salem stairs, and now we have room there for a McIntire sofa. Over it there is a picture of Canton, painted in China about 1800.

In 1961 the children of my friend Mrs. J. Watson Webb wanted to give the Museum the pine dresser and the pink Staffordshire plates which I had seen in her house at Shelburne, Vermont, and which had interested me in collecting American antiques. Where the Visitors' Entrance had been there was now a large space; and this we made into a room where movies can be shown, and at one side we arranged an alcove for the pine dresser. The room is now called the Electra Webb Hall.

By this time the Museum had decided to install air cooling, and the construction work necessary for it became very involved. Nevertheless, we added a little room next to the China Shop, using some woodwork from Smithtown, Long Island, and a large fanlight that had been in the house here at Winterthur. We called this room the China Trade Room, and placed in it a ship captain's day bed, which our friend Mrs. C. Oliver Iselin gave the Museum, and a cane sofa that had been on an American clipper ship, which was given to us by Mrs. J. Stanley Reeve. Also here is some lacquer furniture given to the Museum by Mrs. G. Brooks Thayer.

The air-cooling equipment required several vaults in the ground, and on top of these we were able to build storerooms. This gives us space we needed for rugs and bedspreads; and, as well, we now have a receiving room, a cataloguing room, and a room where a large-scale model of the Museum is displayed and the walls are lined with the many certificates won by the Holsteins of the Winterthur Farm. In the Bedspread Room, which the Museum had outgrown, we are planning to have the Textile Room, where the sample pieces of old textiles can be looked at and studied.

Some rooms in the Museum are being changed around now. The Williams Room, which will have marbleized woodwork from the William Williams house at Lebanon, Connecticut, is replacing the Belle Isle Room because it is the correct woodwork for the furniture there. The Wynkoop Room is being changed slightly, and next to it will be the Shipley Room, which comes from the Shipley house, built about 1750 in Wilmington. On the floor above, a large room has been made out of several workrooms to display an eighteenth-century Baltimore billiard table. Robert Raley, our architect, found some fine Baltimore woodwork in a house about to be torn down, and we were able to use it. We also have two small rooms opening off the Billiard Room, where we are going to have wallpaper painted in Salem, Massachusetts, by Michel Felice Corné. There was a small sun porch opening off this room, and this is going to be a place where visitors may stop and sit down. They can also look at the view from here.

As we have woodwork from an early house in Newport, Rhode Island, we plan to install this paneling in the New York Bedroom. The Newport furniture now in the Hampton Room will be installed in this room, where it will be more appropriate. The furniture in the New York Bedroom will be put in the Hampton Room.

When the South Wing was built, we took part of the Port Royal Façade in the Court for the new entrance, and so we have recently put in its place the south façade of the Banister-MacKaye house at Middletown, Rhode Island, from which the Banister Stair Hall and the Chippendale Bedroom in the South Wing have come. This façade is of rusticated wood and is painted red to match the original color. Now a new entrance hall and a bookshop are being built. Eventually an alcove will be made in Schimmel Hall, so that the hall will have a somewhat more open effect.

1839–1884

1884–1902

1902–1929

1929–1959

Winterthur, 1963

Vauxhall Room (see page 42)

Readbourne Parlor (see page 45)

Port Royal Parlor (see page 64)

Montmorenci Stair Hall (see page 86)

Blackwell Parlor (see page 67)

McIntire Bedroom (see page 89)

Kershner Parlor (see page 166)

Fraktur Room (see page 168)

Seventeenth Century Room

The low-ceiled hall from a house built about 1684 at Essex, Massachusetts, suggests a seventeenth-century New England room. A Massachusetts side chair and a maple Carver chair from Rhode Island flank the recessed fireplace. In the corner hangs a rare wall cupboard. On the painted chest of drawers from the Connecticut River Valley are a Bible box and delft wine bottles. A pine bench stands beside the stretcher-base table, on which are wooden plates, a burl bowl, and a pewter dish attributed to John Dolbeare, of Boston. The only floor covering is a deerskin.

The Seventeenth Century

Colonists coming to America in the seventeenth century brought with them ideas and traditions that were reflected in their buildings and their furniture. The houses of New England were built in the same manner as yeomen's cottages in East Anglia, with heavy oak frames, steep roofs, and small windows with leaded panes; the vagaries of the New England climate demanded that the half-timber walls be covered with weatherboarding, and thus the American clapboard house came into being. Using materials and methods they were accustomed to, Swedish settlers on the Delaware built log cabins, which within two centuries had become the symbol of the American frontier.

Although Renaissance architecture had been introduced to England with the building of the Queen's House at Greenwich before Massachusetts was settled, the earlier traditional forms persisted in the colonies. Multipurpose rooms, such as the main room of Seth Story's house shown on the opposite page, served the same function as the medieval hall and were similarly used for cooking, eating, and even sleeping. Nothing remains of the early furniture of Virginia, and little is known of that of New England before the 1650's; but toward the end of the century craftsmen had established themselves, and the products of such artisans as the joiner Thomas Dennis and the silversmith Jeremiah Dummer have been preserved to this day. Furniture styles followed patterns set in England. Oak was the principal wood used, and in some cases maple and pine. Ornament consisted of applied moldings, incised carving, and often painted decoration. Stools were commonly used for seating, chairs being reserved for the head of the house or for important guests. The most impressive piece of furniture was the court cupboard, used both for storage and for the exhibition of cherished possessions.

Silver, or plate, as it was often described, was a convenient means of preserving and displaying one's wealth; and numerous handsome forms were made in Boston and New York before 1700. Iron utensils were made here, but candlesticks and other fine metal objects had to be imported. To supplement locally produced earthenware, ceramics were brought from abroad; excavations of early settlements have yielded fragments of such European pottery as English and Dutch tin-glazed earthenware and Rhenish stoneware. Some degree of luxury was possible, as suggested by the fact that the inventory made at New Haven of Governor Eaton's possessions, valued at more than £ 1000, included carpets, cushions, curtains, and linens of various descriptions.

Hart Room

Among the New England crafts represented in the Hart Room is a silver tankard made about 1676 by Jeremiah Dummer and owned originally by the Church of Christ in Charlestown, Massachusetts. The oak spice chest, marked T H 1679, belonged to Thomas Hart, son of the builder of the Hart house.

Like the Seventeenth Century Room, the Hart Room was undoubtedly used for more than one purpose. Originally on the second floor of the house built about 1670 by Thomas Hart at Ipswich, Massachusetts, it is arranged to show its possible function as a sitting-bedroom. A similar room from the same house is in the American Wing of the Metropolitan Museum of Art. In construction, the room resembles that from the Story house, with a heavy summer beam supporting the joists in the ceiling. A shouldered, or "gunstock," post in the corner carries the girts, and the window with leaded sash is set between the studs.

With the exception of the late-seventeenth-century gate-leg table from Pennsylvania, all the furniture here is of New England origin, most important of which is the oak court cupboard bearing the initials of its original owners, Ephraim and Hannah Foster, and the date *1684*. It is attributed to Thomas Dennis, the master joiner of Ipswich, and was included in the article Dr. Irving P. Lyon published in *Antiques* in 1938 establishing Dennis as the earliest American furniture craftsman whose product is known. Also thought to be Dennis's work is the spice chest on the trestle-base table beneath the window. The carved wainscot chair at the left also has an Ipswich history, while the joint stool in front of the table represents the most common seating form used in seventeenth-century New England. The silver tankards on top of the court cupboard and the pewter charger and flagon on the lower shelf suggest other New England crafts, while the fact that Englishmen coming to America brought with them treasured possessions from home is indicated by the seal-top silver spoon on the center table. It was once owned by Elder William Brewster, whose name has been given to the type of chair beside the court cupboard. The efforts of the colonists to approximate the comforts of home with imported luxuries are recalled by the delft pottery—wine bottles, puzzle jugs, and posset pots—brass candlesticks, red-and-gold Italian brocatelle at the windows and on the low-post bed, and an Ushak, or "Turkey," carpet on the floor. The warmth provided by such imported materials, coupled with the intimate feeling of the small room, perhaps gave the colonists a sense of security and protection in the wilderness.

Oyster Bay Room

Furnishings from New York and New England are found in the Oyster Bay Room, where the woodwork is from the Job Wright house, built soon after 1667 at Oyster Bay on the north shore of Long Island. The architecture indicates the Dutch and Flemish practice of supporting a deep, narrow summer beam on a protruding vertical post. Oyster Bay had been settled by English colonists during the Dutch occupation of New Netherlands; Job Wright was the son of a Quaker husbandman from New England, and the house he built blends the Dutch and English traditions.

The fireplace is constructed in the English manner; its decorated lintel, from a contemporary house across Long Island Sound in Milford, Connecticut, is the only known American example with carved ornament.

Beneath the window is a Hadley chest, its front surface carved with the foliate design suggestive of tulips found on a number of chests from the Connecticut River Valley; its center panel bears the initials *PW* for Polly Warner, of Harwinton, Connecticut, for whom it was made. On top of the chest is a Bible box and an earthenware jug with the incised motto *If God be for us, ho can be againc us 1667,* which sums up the faith and courage of colonial Americans. Next to the chest is a slat-back chair with large mushroom-shaped terminals on the front posts. In form it contrasts with the wainscot chair found in Southampton, Long Island, and the two side chairs, which, displaying upholstered seats and backs, are generally known as Cromwellian chairs. The chair at the left has its original upholstery of Turkey work, a domestic imitation of the knotted carpets imported into Europe and America from the Near East. A gate-leg table with trestle feet and turned supports stands in the center of the room; in the corner is a similar table with gates closed and leaves folded, indicating the usefulness of convertible furniture in small seventeenth-century houses. Above it hangs a map of New Jersey by John Seller, and at the right is a painting representing Spring, one of a group originally owned in the Hudson Valley by the Van Vooris family. The rug is a seventeenth-century Kuba.

In the Oyster Bay Room is A Mapp of New JARSEY *by John Seller, printed in London shortly after the English conquest of New Netherlands in 1664. Although using a Dutch view of New Amsterdam, it is the first map to bear the name of New York.*

William and Mary Period 1700–1725

When Prince William of Orange and his English wife crossed the Channel in 1688 to assume the British throne, they carried with them Continental tastes in architecture and the decorative arts that had considerable effect upon England and eventually upon America. The style associated with their names was a derivation of baroque design emanating from post-Renaissance Italy, and is marked by bold curved ornament and an interest in the plastic effect of surfaces, with strong contrasts of light and dark.

During the first quarter of the eighteenth century, America reflected this change in taste: the height and sizes of rooms increased; wainscoted walls with raised panels and fireplaces framed by bolection moldings replaced the simple sheathing of the earlier period; leaded casements disappeared as sash windows, first recorded in England in 1685, came into general use; and walls were painted, often marbleized in imitation of the palaces of Italy and France. The woodwork installed in the Thomas Goble house (page 30) is a vigorous, if provincial, example of this technique.

In furniture, heavy forms became lighter. The tops received more attention, as illustrated on this page by the domed hood of the walnut case for a clock by Anthony Ward, of New York. Chairs remained straight and rigid, but there was a tendency toward scrolled or brush-shaped feet, curved arms, and carved and pierced crestings. Leather and caning were common as upholstery. New forms appeared: the couch, or day bed, came into being; the desk developed from a Bible box placed upon a frame; the upholstered chair grew out of the Cromwellian form into the easy chair with wings and rolled arms. The availability of walnut enabled American craftsmen to make use of this close-grained wood, and veneers cut from burled walnut or maple gave richly figured surfaces to chests and desks.

Trade with the Orient had enriched Holland and England, and the porcelains and lacquer work, imported by the East India companies along with tea and spices, affected the arts. The craze for porcelain inspired great collections and the imitation of it by Dutch and English earthenware factories. Delftware, brasses, even silks and damasks, were imported by Americans to add color and richness to their houses.

Morattico Hall

Against a background of woodwork from Morattico, a Virginia house built about 1715, the furnishings illustrate seventeenth-century and William and Mary forms. Earliest is the New England chest decorated with applied moldings. The long bench and the turned stool preserve earlier forms, while the velvet-covered easy chair suggests the new style. The caned chairs with Flemish-scroll feet are English in origin, imported at an early date. American examples of the same form flank the chest. An eighteenth-century map of Pennsylvania hangs above, and on the other wall is a child's portrait attributed to Justus Engelhard Kühn.

Flock Room

The simple splendor of an eighteenth-century Virginia plantation house is suggested by the Flock Room, which takes its name from the green-and-gray wall covering of flocked canvas simulating cut velvet. Traces of the original blue paint remain on much of the woodwork which, like that in Morattico Hall, was formerly in Morattico, built about 1715 on the banks of the Rappahannock River in Richmond County, Virginia. Dominating the room is the fireplace wall with landscapes painted on panels framed by marbleized bolection moldings. The unusual paintings, the vigorous plastic effect of the paneling, and the impressive scale of the room make it one of the outstanding examples of its period in America. Baroque elements appear in the bold pattern of the flock wall covering; in the window hangings inspired by the published designs of Daniel Marot, Prince William's Huguenot architect who followed him to England; and in the spiral-turned legs of the walnut drop-leaf table and of the New York chest-on-frame against the wall. The andirons in the fireplace and the brass candlesticks on top of the chest repeat this design.

New England chairs are arranged in the room. Made of maple and upholstered in leather, they all display turned legs; some of them have brush-shaped Spanish feet. Those with shaped backs illustrate a gradual change in the traditional chair form. A turned stool, painted blue, is drawn up to the table, where a copy of Samuel Willard's *Body of Divinity,* published in Boston in 1726, lies on the velvet cloth. Beside the fireplace is an American easy chair upholstered in gold silk brocatelle. Next to it is an American iron candlestand representative of the "great iron candlesticks" often mentioned in early inventories. In the corner is a couch, or day bed, with cushions on its seat and adjustable back covered in stamped velvet. A large looking glass, its veneered frame enhanced by a pierced cresting, reflects the light of the candles in the Dutch brass chandelier. A late-seventeenth-century Kuba carpet from the Caucasus is on the floor.

The eighteenth-century wall covering in the Flock Room
was achieved by adhering flock, or cut-up wool, to a stenciled
design of shells and leaves on canvas. A staghunt in the grounds
of an unidentified country house is the subject of the overmantel painting. Probably contemporary with the woodwork,
it is considered among the earliest American landscapes.

Walnut Room

From Belle Isle, a house built before 1760 at Litwalton, Lancaster County, Virginia, by William Bertrand, the flat wainscoting of the Walnut Room recalls the oak paneling of rooms in Jacobean England and forms an appropriate background for William and Mary furniture. The paneling, a curious throwback to an earlier style, retains its original light-brown paint, which contrasts with the blue-green mantel and cornice. The trestle-foot bed is of maple and ash, its half canopy so devised that the mattress could be folded against the back curtain when not in use. The hangings are of American crewel, with fanciful patterns embroidered in wool threads on a linen ground. Also an outstanding example of American needlework is the hatchment above the mantel, displaying the arms of Penhallow impaled with Kneeland. It was worked in Portsmouth, New Hampshire, by Prudence Kneeland Penhallow, widow of Deacon Samuel Penhallow. In England, hatchments, usually painted on wooden panels, were hung as memorials in churches. Embroidered examples in this country more often served domestic purposes. Beside the fireplace is a walnut and cane armchair made in New England. Its scrolled arms and arched cresting are characteristic of the William and Mary style; its cabriole legs forecast the coming Queen Anne style. Opposite it is a child's chair made later in the eighteenth century as evidenced by a bow-shaped cresting rail and vasiform splat, but retaining an earlier feature in its Spanish feet. Next to the bed is a maple dressing table grained to imitate walnut. It holds a miniature walnut writing desk, on top of which is a small garniture of blue-and-white earthenware bearing the mark of the De Twee Scheepses factory at Delft. A Spanish-foot side chair, painted black and its seat covered with old red leather, is placed in front of the dressing table, above which hangs a portrait of Mrs. Benjamin Austin, of Boston, painted there by John Greenwood before 1752, when the artist went to Surinam. Dutch and English vases, obelisks, and flower holders decorate the mantelshelf. Delft tiles frame the fireplace opening, in which is a pair of andirons with heavy brass caps. A pair of matching creeper andirons holds the kindling. An Ushak rug dating from the seventeenth century is on the floor.

*Executed in shades of blue, green, red, and yellow, the
crewelwork on the bed in the Walnut Room typifies American
embroidery of the mid–eighteenth century. Birds perched in
a stylized cherry tree formed of woolen threads on a linen
ground are but one of the fanciful designs employed by colonial
needlewomen.*

William and Mary Parlor

The marbleized woodwork of the William and Mary Parlor, painted red, gray, and white, is from the Thomas Goble house at Lincoln, Massachusetts. A Turkish carpet covers the gate-leg table, and the red-painted frame of the looking glass above it reveals, as does most of the furniture in the room, the popularity of painted decoration. The spoon-back side chair next to the fireplace is grained to imitate walnut, and opposite it stands an armchair attributed to John Gaines II, of Ipswich, Massachusetts. Under the window stands a small painted chest from Taunton, Massachusetts, decorated by Robert Crosman and dated *1742*.

Tappahannock Room

In the Tappahannock Room a frieze of small panels distinguishes woodwork once in the Ritchie house, which was built at Tappahannock, Virginia, before 1725. Of particular interest among furniture from the Middle Colonies is the ball-foot chest. Made of walnut and dated *1737*, it is the first piece of American furniture acquired for the Winterthur collection. Above it hangs a looking glass in a walnut frame, its two sections separated by a shaped bar of blue glass. The desk-on-frame and the chair in front of it are both from Pennsylvania, as is the leather-covered armchair, which is attributed to the Moravian colony at Bethlehem. The silk needlework picture above the desk is inscribed *Mary King 1745*. An unusual candlestand, also from Pennsylvania, with adjustable candle arm and round shelf, stands next to the caned armchair.

The Queen Anne Period 1725–1760

Although Queen Anne died in 1714, the decorative style bearing her name flourished in America from about 1725 until 1760, a lag that can be attributed to the conservatism of colonials and to the difficulty in transmitting new ideas across the ocean. During this period a refinement of baroque design took place; the taste for furnishings with bold curves and heavy carving gave way to those of a subtle outline based upon the *cyma recta,* a simple S-curve described by William Hogarth as the "line of beauty." The shell, another device of baroque derivation, became the favorite ornament of American craftsmen and their patrons.

In architecture as well, there was a refinement of baroque taste. The panels of wainscoted walls were no longer raised, but recessed, as at Readbourne (page 44). Rooms began to include pilasters and pedimented doorways as classical elements gained favor.

The S-curved cabriole leg was adopted almost universally; and complementing it, seat frames of chairs were often curved and the backs shaped to fit the human body. Walnut and maple, with an occasional use of mahogany, were the predominant woods. Generally the grain of the wood provided sufficient ornament, but furniture was sometimes embellished with carved shells or foliage. Regional variations developed in the cities along the seacoast. The types of feet found on furniture symbolized the differences: a pad foot in New England; a thick, pointed foot in New York; trifid, carved pad, and slipper feet in Pennsylvania. The claw-and-ball foot came into vogue toward the end of the period.

Most of the popular forms were modifications of those already in use. The sofa evolved from the bench. High chests and secretary desks became more graceful. At least one new form, the tea table, reflected developing social customs.

There was a demand for accessories to go with the furniture made here. Pewter, imported and locally made, was common for table use; and salt-glazed stoneware and Chinese porcelains supplemented delftwares. An interest in the exotic led to the use of Indian chintzes, crewel embroideries, and japanned furniture imitating Oriental lacquer. Gilt sconces and brass candlesticks were imported, but native silversmiths produced a variety of forms. It is not surprising that an Englishman who had visited Boston in 1720 found the people, their houses, their furniture, and their conversation "as splendid and showy as that of the most considerable Tradesman in London."

Tappahannock Hall

The leaf-green woodwork is from the Ritchie house at Tappahannock, Virginia. A Massachusetts Queen Anne table in the center of the room has an Italian marble top, and at the right is a New York armchair covered in plum-colored moreen. Beside it stands a Massachusetts high chest made of butternut with inlaid decoration, dating about 1740. The yellow twill cushion of the Queen Anne day bed is appliquéd with lace and matches the window curtains. A Newport armchair, also upholstered in moreen, stands at the left. English mirrored sconces hang on a wall covered with painted canvas.

Cecil Bedroom

The Cecil Bedroom is from an early-eighteenth-century house at Northeast, in Cecil County, Maryland, where it was a ground-floor parlor. Blue-painted woodwork with raised panels provides a background for New England furniture of the Queen Anne style. A unique pad-foot maple bed from Rhode Island dominates the room. Its tall, slender posts support hangings of mid-eighteenth-century crewel embroidery. The bedcover, an extraordinary combination of floral patterns and applied strapwork in shades of rose, blue, green, and yellow, was originally owned by Thomas Hancock, a Boston merchant and shipowner, and later by his nephew and heir, John Hancock, signer of the Declaration of Independence and Governor of Massachusetts. Curtains of similar embroidered material hang at the window.

A Connecticut side chair of cherry, with straight stiles and a narrow vase-shaped splat, its seat covered with needlework of a flame-stitch pattern, stands in front of a Rhode Island desk dating from about 1750. The shells carved on the short cabriole legs of the desk presage the splendidly carved shells found on later Newport pieces. Beside the desk is an unusual comb-back corner chair, also from Newport. Another Newport chair, with the rounded cresting raii associated with the work of Job Townsend, first of the Townsend–Goddard family of cabinetmakers, is drawn up to a walnut dressing table from Massachusetts. Pincushions and brushes are placed in front of the dressing glass on top of the table. An iron candlestand is at the left of the bed, and next to it stands a mixing table from Massachusetts, its maple frame painted black and its top formed of blue-and-white Delft tiles. In the foreground is a walnut side chair from Newport, featuring the notched vase-shaped splat, horseshoe seat, and pad feet, characteristic of the Queen Anne style in that city. Its seat is covered with a crewelwork design of lambs and dogs in a pastoral setting. Other examples of needlework hang as framed pictures on the walls, and on the floor is a late-seventeenth-century Ushak carpet.

In the Cecil Bedroom is a walnut corner chair made between 1735 and 1750. The needlework picture is traditionally the work of Dorothy Cotton, cousin of the theologian Cotton Mather.

Hardenbergh Parlor

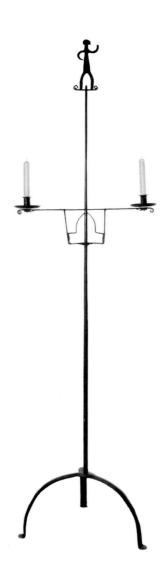

The farm land of the Hudson River Valley, settled by the Dutch in the seventeenth century, prompted Hector St. John de Crève-cœur to ask in his *Letters from an American Farmer,* "Precious soil, I say to myself, by what singular custom of law is it that thou wast made to constitute the riches of the freeholder." The atmosphere of the eighteenth-century agricultural society Crèvecœur so admired is recalled by the planked ceiling, deep beams, and paneled fireplace wall retaining its original gray-blue paint from the farmhouse built by Johannes G. Hardenbergh near Kerhonkson, Ulster County, New York, in 1762. Typical of the stone houses of the upper Hudson Valley, the house has historical significance as well, for it was here that public records were brought from Kingston for safekeeping when the British occupied the valley during the Revolution. A tessellated oilcloth, or painted canvas, a rare survival of a common eighteenth-century floor covering, has been used here. This piece has a New York history. A similar pattern painted on the floor boards was discovered in the restoration of the Van Cortlandt manor house at Croton-on-Hudson.

An outstanding example of the Queen Anne style as expressed in New York is seen in the walnut side chair in the foreground. The shaped rear legs are unusual in New York chairs, as are the rounded stiles and lambrequin carved on the knee. Opposite it stands a New York easy chair, its sturdy walnut cabriole leg and pad foot typical of the region; and behind it is a mahogany tea table having the characteristically pointed pad, or "shod," foot of New York. On the table, which was originally owned by the Stockton family of Princeton, New Jersey, are a pewter teapot and sugar bowl, probably made in Philadelphia, and cups and saucers of English salt-glazed stoneware decorated with incised blue figures and known as *scratch blue*. A needlework picture, depicting Biblical scenes and inscribed *ELizaBeth E LinendorPh Her WorK AGed 10 YearS 1766,* hangs above the fireplace, in which is a pair of Hudson Valley andirons. A copper teakettle hangs from an iron kettle tilter on the swinging crane original to the room. At the right is a Dutch brass fat lamp, and on the hearth a copper chocolate pot, dated *1703,* rests on an iron trivet of probable American origin in which the date *1778* is worked into the design. The American flintlock rifle and the powder horn and pouch are reminders that life in Ulster County was still unsettled in the mid-eighteenth century and Indians roamed the countryside not far to the west.

Among examples of Hudson Valley ironwork in the Hardenbergh Parlor is an early-eighteenth-century candlestand (facing page) found in the Hermanus Mynderse house, which was built in 1743 at Saugerties, New York. Of the many American lighting fixtures in the Winterthur collection, this is of particular interest for its unique finial in the shape of a man.

Hardenbergh Bedroom

A kitchen, a parlor, and a bedroom comprised the ground floor of Johannes G. Hardenbergh's house near Kerhonkson, New York. The woodwork from the bedroom, as well as that of the parlor, has been installed at Winterthur; and an inscribed stone dated *1762* from the wall of the house has been placed above the entrance door. The Hardenberghs were typical of Dutch families in New York. The first to settle there had been merchants in Amsterdam; and in 1708 one of their descendants, Major Johannes Hardenbergh, received a grant from Queen Anne that covered most of the Catskill Mountain range and was known for many years as the Hardenbergh Tract.

Furnishings from the Hudson Valley, simpler than those in the parlor, are displayed in the bedroom. The bed is hung with a valance and curtains of eighteenth-century blue-and-white resist-dyed cotton, an English material popular along the Hudson and on Long Island. An unusual blanket employing the same colors and designs covers the bed. It bears the name of Mary Foot and the date *A.D. 1778*. Hanging on the wall at the left of the bed is a clock of the Friesland type often found in Dutch interiors. Continental in derivation is the kas, a two-door cupboard of a kind found in New York and New Jersey and, in a variety of styles, in Pennsylvania, where it was more akin to German and Swiss antecedents. The example here is distinguished by its grisaille decoration, reminiscent of *trompe l'œil* painting in Dutch houses of the seventeenth century. On top of the kas is a large blue-and-white Delft garniture.

Rush-seated chairs, broad and comfortable in their proportions, were advertised in Albany newspapers as "fiddleback" chairs until the late eighteenth century. The large armchair standing beside a turned stool is grained to imitate walnut, while the red-painted side chair is decorated with a heart-shaped piercing in the splat. Both have the trumpet-shaped legs and pad feet characteristic of Hudson Valley "fiddlebacks." The American flax wheel, fitted with old tow, was originally used in the Hardenbergh house. The unusual cradle, painted green and yellow and neatly suspended in a turned trestle-foot frame, is also from the Hudson Valley and holds a wooden-headed doll. The rug is a colorful example of European needlework of the late eighteenth century.

Originally used in the Hardenbergh house, the flax wheel
is made of maple, cherry, and ash, and dates from about 1780.
Its turned legs resemble those on contemporary Windsor chairs.
The Hardenbergh house (right) was a one-story stone structure
overlooking Rondout Creek near Kerhonkson, New York.
The center door led to the bedroom.

Queen Anne Dining Room

The Queen Anne Dining Room presents a picture of the good living the modern romantic associates with the eighteenth century. Here New York furniture of the Queen Anne style is displayed in a paneled room from a mid-eighteenth-century house at East Derry, New Hampshire. The woodwork has been restored to its original green color; and stop-fluted pilasters flank a recessed fireplace bordered by English delft tiles decorated in purple, blue, and white. A grate within the fireplace holds chunks of coal, and at the right is a brass plate warmer.

Grouped around the oval walnut table is a rare set of upholstered armchairs covered with resist-dyed cotton of a blue-and-white pomegranate design related to contemporary damask patterns. Originally owned by the Tibbits family of New York, the chairs show cabriole legs ending in pad feet. In contrast, the legs of the table, an heirloom of the Beekman family, end in the pointed shod foot characteristic of New York at this time. In the background, side chairs with solid splats and carved cresting rails, similar to chairs owned by Stephanus Van Cortlandt, flank a Dutchess County kas, which retains its original green paint. The arched panel in the door is a motif often found in architecture and furniture of the Queen Anne style.

The table is set with English pistol-handled knives and forks, and spoons made for the Deutch family by Lewis Fueter, a Swiss-born silversmith who was working in New York by 1769. The large Bristol delft punch bowl, inscribed *George Skinner, Boston, 1732,* holds a punch ladle marked by Simeon Soumain, of New York. At each place is an English delft plate decorated in a manner similar to the fireplace tiles and the bowls on top of the kas and attributed to the pottery at Wincanton. Also on the table is a pewter tankard by Joseph Leddell and various pewter mugs, the work of Frederick Bassett, Samuel Pierce, and Ebenezer Southmayd. A brass chandelier hangs above the table, and a seventeenth-century Ushak rug covers the floor.

*In the Queen Anne Dining Room the pewter tankard
(opposite page) by Joseph Leddell, of New York, represents
the earliest American tankard form. The carved fish—a smelt,
a mackerel, and a cod—are suspended in a gilded shadowbox
formerly owned in Plymouth, Massachusetts.*

Vauxhall Room

The unpainted pine paneling on the fireplace wall of the Vauxhall Room is from Vauxhall Gardens, the home of Thomas Maskell at Greenwich—once called Cohansie—in the southern part of New Jersey. The first section of the house was built about 1700; this room was in a brick addition of about 1725. A heavy bolection molding and seventeenth-century Delft tiles frame the fireplace, which is copied from one in the contemporary Amstel House at New Castle, Delaware. Ventilating grilles, such as those above the closet doors, are seen occasionally in South Jersey houses.

As early as 1697 semiannual fairs were held at Greenwich, and it was customary for merchants to come there from Philadelphia. Thus it is appropriate that Philadelphia furniture of the Queen Anne style is here arranged as in a parlor, or common room, the term used in the inventory of Thomas Maskell's estate. At the walnut drop-leaf table, of probable Virginia origin, are chairs featuring the trifid feet, shell-carved knees, and vase-shaped splats, typical of Philadelphia work of this period. The armchair in the foreground descended in a Bound Brook, New Jersey, family. From Philadelphia or Maryland and dating from about 1750 is the handsome walnut high chest of drawers, owned originally by Christopher Marshall, a Philadelphia Quaker and member of the Council of Safety in 1777.

An eighteenth-century Dutch chandelier provides light for the table, where French candlesticks and English delft bowls flank a brass monteith hung with wineglasses. Other lighting fixtures include a Hudson Valley candlestand with an elaborately scrolled bracket, at the left of the fireplace, and brass sconces on the frame of the New York chimney looking glass. Reflected in this glass is a

The quality of Philadelphia craftsmanship is epitomized by a walnut armchair in the Vauxhall Room. The delft bowl on the table (also shown on the far right) was probably made at Bristol, England; also of English manufacture is the brass monteith used for chilling wineglasses.

42

mantel garniture with polychrome decoration, bearing the mark of the Delft pottery known as *De Pauw* (The Peacock).

The rug is an Ushak weave, dating about 1700; and the walls are covered with English flocked canvas, unusual in having an architectural dado incorporated in the design. Its effect is similar to that of the cut velvet on the chair seats. Such luxuries suggest the efforts of the colonists to keep abreast of the styles in England, as does the iron fireback in the fireplace, which displays the royal coat of arms and motto *Honi soit qui mal y pense* and was made in 1747 at the Oxford Furnace in Warren County, New Jersey.

Readbourne Parlor

"Quillwork," elaborately fashioned of rolled paper on wire frames and sprinkled with mica, forms the background of the sconces in the Readbourne Parlor, owned and presumably made by Elizabeth Hunt Wendell, who married Parson Thomas Smith, of Portland, Maine, in 1766. The original silver candle arms are marked by Jacob Hurd, of Boston, with the die he used between 1729 and 1740.

The Readbourne Parlor was originally in the house near Centre-ville, Maryland, built in 1733 by Colonel James Hollyday and considered to be the first "mansion" in the colony. A corner fireplace is enhanced by a bolection molding and seventeenth-century Dutch tiles around the opening. The fully paneled walls, customary in early-eighteenth-century America, have been painted a gray-white.

The furniture complements the architecture in quality. Arranged here are Philadelphia chairs of the Queen Anne style with trifid, carved pad, and claw-and-ball feet. The sofa, also from Philadelphia and an early example of the form, has cabriole legs ending in carved pad feet, as well as flat stretchers, a rare feature in Pennsylvania furniture. Like the easy chair adjacent to it, it is covered in eighteenth-century Italian brocatelle of a blue compatible with the color of the rich velvet curtains and the dress of Experience Johnson Gouverneur, whose portrait, painted by John Wollaston about 1750, hangs above the fireplace. The tea table, probably made for Dr. Thomas Graeme, of Graeme Park, near Philadelphia, reflects the fact that tea, introduced into Europe in the early seventeenth century, reached genuine popularity in the Queen Anne period, calling into being new social customs and attendant forms in furniture and ceramics. Thus on the table are cups, saucers, a teapot, and cream pot of salt-glazed stoneware colorfully decorated in imitation of Chinese porcelains. Also illustrating the European concept of Oriental elegance is the japanned case of the clock made by Gawen Brown, who was working in Boston in 1749. The frame of the looking glass above the sofa is still another example of japanned decoration, which involved the use of gesso, gold leaf, and varnish on a painted ground to achieve the effect of Chinese lacquer.

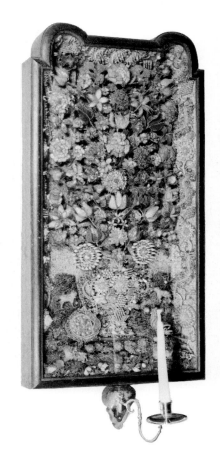

The quillwork sconces on either side of the looking glass provide glittering backgrounds for the light from the candles in the silver candle arms attached to them and add a brilliant note to the room, as does the Irish silver chandelier, which was made about 1742 and installed as a memorial in a church in Galway. Other silver candle-holders in the room are the pair of wall sconces, made in 1718 by John Sanders, of London, and the American candlesticks on the tea table, engraved with the arms of Peter Faneuil and bearing the mark of Nathaniel Morse, who worked in Boston from 1709 until 1748. The rugs are finely woven Ispahans, made in Persia in the late sixteenth century.

Readbourne Stair Hall

The stair hall at Readbourne formed the central passage of the house. The archway led to the stairs; another one, balancing it, led to the parlor. Philadelphia side chairs, transitional in design between the Queen Anne and the approaching Chippendale taste, flank a Maryland high chest of drawers. Its companion dressing table is also in the Winterthur collection. Chinese export porcelain bowls are displayed in the cupboard, in front of which a walnut candlestand with an unusual shelf and screen stands between Philadelphia armchairs. A seventeenth-century Persian carpet, often described as a "Goa" rug, lies on the floor.

Queen Anne Bedroom

The Queen Anne Bedroom was originally the rear chamber in a house in Coombs' Alley, Philadelphia, built about 1760 by Henry Harrison and rented by John Barker, a tailor. Beside the walnut low-post bed, dating from about 1760, is a Chester County spice chest. An arm-chair of the type attributed to William Savery stands at the left. The cradle and pad-foot stool are probably of New Jersey origin. Hanging on the wall are a water color of Philadelphia, painted in 1735 by George Wood, and a print showing the Pennsylvania Hospital, by James Claypoole, Jr., published in 1761.

The Chippendale Period 1760–1790

In 1754 the London cabinetmaker Thomas Chippendale published *The Gentleman and Cabinet-Maker's Director;* and although he was merely recording the current fashions, his name is now given to the furniture style shown in the engraved illustrations in his book. Copies reached America by 1760; and while American craftsmen tended toward less flamboyant interpretations of the designs, they offered their customers furniture in what Chippendale considered to be the "Gothic, Chinese, and Modern taste" until about 1790. The modern taste reflected a decorative movement, French in origin and usually described as "rococo," which emphasized light and delicate ornament incorporating such elements as pierced shells, leaves, and flowers arranged in asymmetrical compositions. In furniture the claw-and-ball foot was the common ending for cabriole legs. Pierced splats and bow-shaped cresting rails gave pattern and lightness to chair backs, as demonstrated by the Massachusetts side chair on this page. Tables and chairs in the "Chinese taste," which called for straight legs and carved fretwork, offered a balance to the curved forms of the French style.

Colonial architecture was conservative, and rococo forms were confined to moldings and carved ornament. Following carpenters' handbooks, such as Batty Langley's *Builder's Treasury,* Americans built in the neo-Palladian style, which had been popular in England early in the century. The façades of most houses were plain and symmetrical, while interior embellishments were concentrated on the fireplace walls of the parlors. English and Chinese wallpapers were popular.

At this time, especially in Philadelphia, the high chest of drawers was perfected as an American furniture form. Native artists came into their own as prosperous colonials sat for such painters as Peale and Copley. Silversmiths enriched their products with engraved or *repoussé* designs following fashionable rococo patterns. Americans continued to import luxury goods; but they were also aware of their own capacities, and a feeling of independence was developing among them, as indicated by the advice Captain Samuel Morris gave his nephew in 1765: "Household goods may be had here as cheap and as well made from English patterns." Within ten years the Battle of Concord took place.

Bowers Parlor

A conservative room of the Chippendale period is the Bowers Parlor
from the house built in the 1760's by Jerathmael Bowers at Somerset,
Massachusetts. Contrasting with the ocher color of the paneled wall
is the blue-and-white Delft garniture on the mahogany mantelshelf.
A leather-upholstered easy chair beside the fireplace faces a
Philadelphia armchair, which, like the Rhode Island side chair at
the left, has the straight leg often seen in Chippendale furniture.
Massachusetts side chairs (also see facing page) flank the chimney
breast. The silvered dial of the cherry tall clock is inscribed by
Daniel Burnap, of East Windsor, Connecticut.

Banister Stair Hall

Hanging in the Banister Stair Hall is an engraving,
The Continence of Scipio, *after Van Dyck, printed in*
London in 1766, but framed and sold by Robert Kennedy,
of Philadelphia.

Only a mile from Newport, the Banister-MacKaye house was built in 1756 as the country residence of John Banister, a prominent merchant whose far-flung interests included land speculation in North Carolina and ships engaged in the African and West Indies trade. Banister had come to Newport from Boston about 1735 and had married Hermione Pelham, the granddaughter of Governor Arnold. Merchant, shipbuilder, privateer, and slave trader, Banister prospered in the triangle trade and brought into Newport such luxuries as glassware, pottery, and textiles. His country house was a large, rusticated wooden building commanding a view of Narragansett Bay. A central hall extended through the house, divided in the characteristic Rhode Island manner by an archway framing the stairs, as in the Vernon and Hunter houses still standing in Newport. The paneled arch, supported on carved corbels, now forms the entrance to the Banister Stair Hall, where the olive color of the woodwork matches traces of the original paint. The doors, trim, and handrail are stained to imitate walnut, also matching the original; the steps retain their old marbleizing, painted in buff and gray.

The mahogany breakfast table at the left illustrates the Chippendale style as expressed in Newport. This particular piece shows a cabriole leg ending in long claws which grasp an oval ball, a feature found in the documented work of John Goddard, one of the early members of the Townsend-Goddard family of craftsmen who dominated the furniture trade in Newport through three generations. The mid-eighteenth-century chairs at either side of the table represent a Newport type combining the solid splat of the Queen Anne style with the claw-and-ball feet found in the Chippendale period. The shells carved on the cresting rail and the knees of the legs are typical of Newport. Above the table is an English engraving mounted on canvas and sold in Philadelphia by Robert Kennedy, whose trade card pasted on the back notifies his customers that he frames and glazes pictures. As the Frenchman Du Simitiere, who visited Newport, mentioned seeing engravings in the Banister house, it is appropriate that prints should be in the hall, where an English lamp lights the room, and fire buckets, containing large linen bags used for rescuing valuable objects, hang from nails driven into the cornice molding. A Ghiordes prayer rug is on the floor.

Chippendale Bedroom

Among the Rhode Island furniture in the Chippendale Bedroom is a mahogany-and-gilt looking glass which dates from the 1770's. A paper label (facing page) pasted to the pine backboard reads: Made by John Townsend, NewPort. *It is one of two looking glasses known to bear the label of a Newport craftsman.*

The Chippendale Bedroom, from the Banister-MacKaye house at Middletown, not far from Newport, Rhode Island, indicates the eighteenth-century practice of using a bedroom as a sitting room, although the bed is not shown in this view. As was customary in New England houses of the period, the fireplace wall is fully paneled and a dado extends around the other three walls. A bolection molding frames the plastered fireplace opening. The hearth is formed of marble blocks, recorded in John Banister's accounts as "marble tiles for the chamber hearth."

A Newport easy chair with flat stretchers and claw-and-ball feet is covered with a green woolen fabric popular for upholstery in the colonies. On the three-legged Rhode Island table beside it is a pewter tankard by Benjamin Day, who died in Newport in 1757, and a copy of *Alciphron ... an Apology for the Christian Religion,* written at Newport by George Berkeley, the Irish clergyman and philosopher who lived there from 1729 until 1731. Next to the fireplace is a dwarf tall clock, its works by Thomas Claggett, of Newport, and its case probably by a member of the Townsend–Goddard family. The pair of side chairs, with pierced splats characteristic of the Chippendale style in Newport and with their original needlework seats, were heirlooms in the Bangs family of Newport. The block-front chest of drawers descended through the Minturn and West families of Bristol, Rhode Island. It is an admirable example of the block-front form that was perfected in Newport and is considered one of the significant American contributions to furniture design. Similarities to a chest labeled by Edmund Townsend suggest that this piece also was made in his shop. The looking glass above the chest is labeled by John Townsend, cousin of Edmund; and the unusual mahogany basin stand beside the chest is attributed to him.

Ball-finial brass andirons, a type often found in Rhode Island, are in the fireplace; and above it hangs an English print, *The Farm Yard,* after Peter de Laër. The mezzotint portrait of Samuel Adams at the right is by Samuel Okey, an English engraver who came to Newport in 1773. Vivid blues and reds in the Turkish carpet offset the soft green of the woodwork.

Chestertown Room

One of the choice pieces of Newport furniture in the Chestertown Room is the mahogany kettle stand attributed to John Townsend. The pierced gallery and the incised carving on the tray mark it as his work. The early Sheffield-plate tea urn, dating from about 1780, has a pineapple-shaped finial, often considered a symbol of hospitality.

Formerly in a house on Water Street in Chestertown, Maryland, the woodwork in the Chestertown Room dates from about 1762 and features such refinements as sunk panels, dentil moldings, and a mahogany chair rail. Hanging within the tabernacle frame of the overmantel is an oil sketch, done in 1789 by Edward Savage, for a portrait of the Washington family. English transfer-printed tiles produced at John Sadler's factory in Liverpool frame the fireplace opening.

Although Chestertown was an active port in the eighteenth century, little furniture is known to have been made there or in the other towns of Maryland's Eastern Shore; and the furnishings of this room are largely of New England origin. The breakfast table in the center of the room bears the label of John Townsend, of Newport. Its stop-fluted legs and fretwork stretchers show his interpretation of the Chinese Chippendale style. The kettle stand next to the table displays the same fretwork in its gallery, and the card table at the right has stop-fluted legs and pierced brackets. Both pieces have been attributed to Townsend. Also believed to be from his shop is the mahogany block-front chest of drawers in the corner. The chairs in front of the fireplace are of Massachusetts origin; the one on the left, originally owned by the Davenport family of Newburyport, is probably the work of Joseph Short, who lived there from 1771 until 1819. Beneath the window is a stool made in New York, and the looking glass at the right was the gift of Martha Washington to Mrs. John E. Van Alen, whose husband was congressman from Rensselaer County, New York.

Worcester porcelain cups and saucers, decorated with scenes after engravings by Robert Hancock, are arranged on the breakfast table. The silver there is of American origin and includes a tray made by Thomas Edwards, of Boston; a teapot by Jacob Hurd; a cream pot and sugar bowl by William Gilbert, of New York; and a footed beaker by Samuel Casey, who lived at South Kingston, Rhode Island. Among imported accessories in the room are the English enamel candlesticks on the chest of drawers and Derby porcelain vases on the card table. The chandelier and the candelabra on the mantel are of English cut glass. Yellow damask curtains, fashioned according to a design in Chippendale's *Director,* hang at the window. A seventeenth-century Ushak carpet is on the floor.

New England Kitchen

Among the objects of everyday life displayed in the New
England Kitchen is a mortar and pestle (far right) in the
Connecticut Valley cupboard. Turned of maple, it is inscribed
TD for Thomas Danforth III, a Connecticut pewterer.
The grease pan (right), used to catch drippings from the meat
on the spit, was an implement essential to open-fire cooking.

Based on the kitchen of a house built at Oxford, Massachusetts, about 1740, the New England Kitchen displays cooking and eating equipment apt to be found in a mid-eighteenth-century American home. A turkey roasting on the spit in the open fireplace represents the common method of cooking; at the left is the oven. The sheathed wall is embellished with fielded panels above the granite lintel of the fireplace. All the woodwork is a deep-red color, often seen in New England.

In houses of this date the kitchen usually extended across the rear of the building, with small rooms at each end to be used for storage and sleeping. The multitude of activities taking place in such a room is suggested by the variety of domestic objects here. A pine and birch chair table, painted red, stands in the center of the room; and spread out on its top are an earthenware colander, a walnut rolling pin, steel sugar nippers, a funnel, and other necessary household implements. Near the edge of the table is a pewter porringer made by Josiah Keene, of Providence, Rhode Island, and placed where it might have been used by a child in the green-painted Windsor high chair. The turnings of the legs and arm supports are characteristic of New England chairs of this type. On the opposite side of the table a brace-back Windsor armchair, probably from Connecticut, stands in front of a Connecticut Valley cupboard, the shelves of which hold earthenware plates, pewter dishes, and small wooden bowls. A pot of dried herbs rests on a table from Ipswich, Massachusetts; the open door leading to a pantry, or buttery, reveals such storage facilities as stoneware jugs, cheese baskets, and a group of English delft jars originally owned in Leicester, Massachusetts.

An American rifle, its stock fashioned of curly maple, hangs above the fireplace. Below it is a long-handled spoon dated *1794* and inscribed with the initials of its original owner, Abigail Whiting, of Wrentham, Massachusetts. A wrought-iron peel, used to remove bread from the oven, leans against the wall; and on the stone hearth, a copper teakettle rests on a brazier. The handle of the kettle is stamped *Oat & Cook,* the mark of Jesse Oat and John Cooke, who advertised in Philadelphia from 1794 until 1798. Also on the hearth is a bell-metal posnet, or footed pot, made in 1730 by Lawrence Langworthy, of Newport, Rhode Island. The device attached to the wall above the fireplace is a clock jack, which, by means of a weight and pulley, made the spit revolve in front of the fire.

Simsbury Room

The bottle chest (facing page), not visible in the photograph above, was made to look like a block-front chest of drawers. Its cherry wood, cabriole legs, and claw-and-ball feet suggest a Connecticut origin. Above it hangs a small mahogany looking glass labeled by James Stokes, of Philadelphia, who maintained a shop there between 1791 and 1804.

Such urban centers in eighteenth-century America as Boston, Newport, New York, and Philadelphia were able to support the craftsmen and their patrons who determined the standards for architecture and the decorative arts in the surrounding areas. Between these cities were sparsely settled regions of farms and small towns where the craftsmen, without the means of knowing the latest fashions in England, developed individual variations within the current styles. Connecticut was typical of such areas. Craftsmen in towns such as Colchester, Hartford, and Windsor, midway between Newport and New York, were influenced by the styles of both centers, but added flourishes of their own invention to give their furniture both a regional and a personal character.

The Simsbury Room suggests the provincial appeal of Connecticut architecture and furniture. From the Goodwin house, built about 1760 in Simsbury, a small town west of Hartford, the paneling here is unusual in having flat fields, probably intended to receive a covering of paper or cloth. An eighteenth-century English chintz has been used to replace the vanished original. Repeating the plastic effect of the paneled dado is the paneled summer beam, which is a refinement of an early structural form. Liverpool tiles showing transfer-printed portraits of English actors and actresses in costume border the fireplace. The plays represented by the tiles were familiar to Americans; and one of the actresses shown, Mrs. Wrighten, who was in America between 1792 and 1796, played in Boston, Philadelphia, New York, and Charleston.

A Connecticut side chair made about 1800 is placed beside a walnut bird-cage tea table, upon which is a tea set of creamware decorated in the pattern popularly known as *Leeds Rose*. Facing the table is an easy chair covered in old mulberry velvet, its tapered front legs indicating a date late in the Chippendale period. Beside it is a cherry kettle stand remarkably like the Newport stand in the Chestertown Room (page 54). Both the stand and the bottle chest in the room reveal the strong influence of Newport styles upon the furniture made in eastern Connecticut. The kettle stand holds a Chinese enamel teapot dating from the late eighteenth century.

Within the fireplace are late-eighteenth-century brass andirons of a type found in Connecticut. A brass-and-copper brazier rests on the hearth. The rug is a Turkish weave dating from the mid-eighteenth century.

Bertrand Room

The Bertrand Room takes its name from William Bertrand, who built Belle Isle at Litwalton, Virginia, the source of the unusually high dado with a frieze of panels above the chair rail. The woodwork in the Walnut Room (page 28) is also from Belle Isle, which dates from sometime before 1760. Painted a cream color, the paneling is a foil for the dark-painted mantel from a later house, Springfield, in Montgomery County, Maryland. An exotic touch is added by the chinoiserie figures on the eighteenth-century Bristol delft tiles outlining the fireplace.

The furniture, mostly of New York origin, is upholstered in red moreen, an eighteenth-century woolen material calendered to give a watered effect. At the five-legged New York gaming table in the center of the room are side chairs, part of an original set of twelve belonging to Stephen Van Rensselaer, last patroon of the Manor in Albany. The distinctive feature of their design is a carved tassel and ruffle in the pierced splat. An armchair from the same set, with carved birds' heads terminating the shaped arms, stands at the right of the fireplace. Facing it is a Newport easy chair showing the vertically rolled arms associated with New England chairs of this type. Flanking a richly carved mahogany tea table found in Albany are side chairs once owned by Sir William Johnson, colonial superintendent of Indian Affairs in New York, and used by him at his fortified mansion, Johnson Hall, near Johnstown. The chairs are attributed to Gilbert Ash, a New York chairmaker; in the corner is a chair with an identical splat, its rear seat rail inscribed and dated by Ash.

Complementing the red chair seats are the red satin curtains at the window, the red and brown tones in the rare Exeter carpet, which dates from about 1760, and a colored engraving printed on glass showing Sir William Johnson in his scarlet coat. Other pictures in the room include a portrait of Mrs. Abraham Jarvis (Ann Farmer), painted by John Durand in New York about 1770; an allegorical mezzotint by Charles Willson Peale of William Pitt; and, over the mantel, an English engraving after Salvator Rosa, framed and sold in Philadelphia.

Among the furniture in the Bertrand Room is a side chair inscribed Made by Gilbert Ash in Wall Street ... April 1756. *Documenting the work of Ash, it records an early date for the Chippendale style in New York.*

Port Royal Entrance Hall

Port Royal, a country house built in 1762 on Frankford Creek, north of Philadelphia, was named after his birthplace by Edward Stiles, a planter and merchant from Port Royal, Bermuda, who had prospered in the West Indies trade. In the original house the staircase was concealed at the left, allowing an unbroken view through the center hall from the front door to the garden, and the same effect is achieved here. The cornice follows the pattern of a Doric entablature, while the arched fanlight of the doorway suggests the pierced shells often seen in ornament of the Chippendale period. A paneled dado skirts the lower wall; above it eighteenth-century Chinese wallpaper, painted in muted shades of green, white, and rose, blends harmoniously with the original gray tones of the woodwork.

Boldly proportioned furniture complements the scale of the architecture. At the left is a New York side table made of mahogany, with an inset top of gray marble. Designs for a "sideboard table" with similar pierced fretwork brackets were included in all three editions of Chippendale's *Director*. Flanking the table are Philadelphia armchairs comparable, perhaps, to the "6 hansom walnut Chairs, open backs Crow feet, and a Shell on the back and on each knee" taken from the house of Mrs. Henry Drinker in 1779 for failure to pay a Continental tax. Also from Philadelphia is the arched-back sofa at the far end of the hall. Its slip cover is made of an eighteenth-century English arborescent chintz. The same material is used on the chair seats. Hanging above the sofa is one of a pair of looking glasses with walnut-veneered frames embellished by gilded carving. They were once in the Bromfield-Phillips house on Beacon Street in Boston, where Abigail Phillips and Josiah Quincy were married in 1769, and have since had a long history of ownership in the Quincy family. Flanking the door are two of the eight gilt wall sconces in the hall that suggest the delicate designs of Thomas Johnson, of London, who published his drawings in 1761.

The *famille rose* porcelain on the side table represents one of the patterns brought from the Orient by way of Europe before American ships traded directly with the East. In the foreground is a large Kuba carpet with a blue ground; beyond it is a late-eighteenth-century Agra carpet from India.

Seen against the Chinese wallpaper in the Port Royal
Entrance Hall is a gilded metal sconce (facing page) of
English origin. The asymmetrically shaped backplate and the
candle cups seemingly formed of gilded leaves are perfect
expressions of rococo design in metal.

Port Royal Parlor

In the Port Royal Parlor, where the woodwork is also from Edward Stiles' house at Frankford, north of Philadelphia, the projecting chimney breast gives the importance of a portico to the fireplace and pedimented overmantel. In this composition freely combined classical elements, including Doric pilasters and a pitch pediment, form a setting for a painting of American ships off Dover by Dominic Serres, a French artist who became marine painter to King George III. The crossetted corners of the tabernacle frame are repeated in the fireplace molding, which holds a liner of marble quarried in Chester County near Philadelphia.

Flanking the fireplace is an unusual pair of Philadelphia sofas, distinguished by cabriole legs ending in claw-and-ball feet. They have historical interest in that they were owned by John Dickinson, a Philadelphia lawyer whose *Letters from a Farmer in Pennsylvania,* published in 1768, expressed the colonial viewpoint toward unjust taxation. Between the sofas is a rare oval stool made in Philadelphia. Carved mahogany candlestands, one from Philadelphia and one probably made in Charleston, hold English candlesticks of paktong, an alloy of nickel, zinc, and copper, often used in place of silver. Beside the tea table at the right is a side chair ranked among the finest of Philadelphia origin. Crisply carved foliage on the knees and in the splat gives brilliance to the chair; it is further enhanced by pendant garlands carved on the stiles and cresting rail. Comparable in elegance of design and in the quality of its carved details is the high chest at the end of the room. Its matching dressing table stands in the corner, and above it hangs an impressive American looking glass of walnut veneer ornamented with gilded carving. At the left of the fireplace is a small marble-topped side table holding English pottery figures of Benjamin Franklin, Philadelphia's most distinguished citizen. Chinese export porcelain bowls line the mantelshelf; and at either end are cut-glass candelabra made in England, as was the glass-and-ormolu chandelier.

The warm gray tones of the walls and woodwork provide a subtle background for the highly colored English carpet, which was woven about 1765 and is an important example of the rococo designs produced by English textile manufacturers. The floral silk curtains are probably of French origin; and slip covers of eighteenth-century green damask have been used on the sofas and chairs, complementing the colors of the rug.

*In the Port Royal Parlor is a handsome mahogany high
chest of drawers (also see facing page)—popularly called a
highboy—demonstrating the elaborate Chippendale style
associated with Philadelphia and made there in 1769 for
Michael Gratz. It illustrates the American development of a
form that is unknown in English furniture of this period.*

Blackwell Parlor

The Blackwell Parlor, originally in a house at 224 Pine Street, Philadelphia, is an outstanding example of eighteenth-century American architecture. Flanked by pedimented doorways, the richly carved chimney breast dominates the room and provides a setting for a landscape painting by Francis Guy, of Perry Hall, an estate near Baltimore. The Philadelphia furniture here represents the highest skills of pre-Revolutionary American craftsmen. Hairy-paw feet, rarely seen in American furniture, occur on the fire screen, on the easy chair next to the fireplace, and on the extraordinary "sample" chair which stands near the mahogany side table and is attributed to Benjamin Randolph. Between the windows is a white-and-gold looking glass originally owned by the Cadwalader family of Philadelphia. An Irish cut-glass chandelier hangs above an unusual piecrust table, beside which is an easy chair with a carved skirt and arms. On the wall are portraits attributed to Thomas McIlworth. The rug is a Kuba weave of the mid-eighteenth century.

Chinese Parlor

Although Americans had no direct trade with China until 1784, they were aware of the Chinese products imported from the Orient in English ships and of the interpretations of Chinese art forms published by English and Continental designers. In the Chinese Parlor, wallpaper painted in China about 1770 and showing scenes of daily life in an Oriental village provides a fitting background for furniture in what the Westerners called the "Chinese taste." The soft colors of the paper are complemented by the eighteenth-century green damask chair covers and window curtains.

At the right is an armchair, one of a set of chairs in the room attributed to the Philadelphia cabinetmaker Benjamin Randolph, who advertised "Chairwork… in the Chinese and Modern Tastes." Grouped around the Newport gaming table in front of the window are chairs attributed to another Philadelphia chairmaker, James Gillingham, who used Plate XIII of Chippendale's *Director* as a guide in fashioning the chair backs. The Newport sofa beside the fireplace is inscribed *Made by Adam S Coe April 1812 for Edw. W. Lawton,* indicating that the appeal of the Chinese Chippendale style lasted for many years. Also an example of the lingering taste for the rococo is the silver teakettle made by Edward Lownes, of Philadelphia, about 1815. It is placed on a carved stand from Charleston, South Carolina. Carved fretwork embellishes the skirt and legs of the Charleston table at the right of the sofa, and the Philadelphia side chair beside it exhibits Chinese pretensions in its straight legs, rail below the seat, and pagoda-like terminals to the posts.

Actually made in China are two sections of a black-and-gold lacquer screen brought to Salem, Massachusetts, before 1800 for Elias Hasket Derby, one of the first Americans to engage in the China trade. The Chinese export porcelain in the shell cupboard is known as *penciled ware* and, dating from about 1730, depicts Western figures in black on a white ground. Philadelphia-made andirons in the fireplace show Chinese influence in their pagoda-shaped finials. The mantel is from the Blackwell house in Philadelphia, and arranged on its shelf is a garniture of Derbyshire spar, resembling one advertised in 1791 by Joseph Anthony as "Derbyshire petrifaction, very elegant." A large Feraghan carpet woven about 1800 covers the floor, and an English cut-glass chandelier lights the center of the room.

Among the furniture in the Chinese Parlor, set against a background of eighteenth-century Chinese wallpaper, is a rare Newport gaming table with French scroll feet, here arranged for whist.

Philadelphia Bedroom

Chinoiserie is the term now applied to seventeenth- and eighteenth-century art forms that corresponded not to actual Chinese objects, but to an image Europeans had of China, the Chinese, and their arts. Thus charming Meissen figures, garden houses on English estates, and even latticework balustrades on American stairways reflect the romantic interest in China that can be traced as far back as the writings of Marco Polo. "Chinese Chippendale" furniture, as shown in the Chinese Parlor on the preceding page, is one expression of this interest. Another is the use in England and America of wallpapers made for export by the Chinese, who obligingly supplied the Western demand. Such a paper, dating from the late eighteenth century, covers the walls of the Philadelphia Bedroom and shows exotic birds in a setting of tree peonies, chrysanthemums, and cherry blossoms against a gray-blue background.

This room suggests the elegance of eighteenth-century Philadelphia; and the skill of the cabinetmakers there is represented by the small chest of drawers at the right of the bed, which bears this label of William Savery: "All Sorts of Chairs and Joiners Work Made and Sold by *William Savery,* At the Sign of the Chair, a little be-low the Market, in Second Street. Philadelphia." Savery was in business between 1742 and 1787, producing during that time furniture for many prominent Philadelphians. Because a dressing table from his shop was the first labeled piece of Philadelphia furniture to be published, his name was for many years synonymous with Philadelphia furniture. Subsequent study has identified other craftsmen whose fame now equals his. The early walnut bed is distinguished by tall, slender posts supported by cabriole legs with shells carved on the knees. It is similar to a bed illustrated in the *Blue Book, Philadelphia Furniture,* by William M. Hornor, Jr., which focused attention on the skills of the eighteenth-century Philadelphia furniture craftsmen. The stand beside the bed, also from Philadelphia, holds an English silver-plated candlestick. A brass chandelier, made in England about 1780, hangs from the ceiling, casting light on a mid-seventeenth-century Kuba rug.

Through the door can be seen the Philadelphia Hall, where the fret-carved woodwork in the Chinese taste is from the Solomon Engels house in Philadelphia and the walls are covered with embroidered silk wall hangings, probably French, but made in imitation of Chinese wallpaper. A Philadelphia side chair stands next to a drop-leaf table on which is a porcelain pagoda, another item made in China to complement the Western image of the Orient.

A fanciful blue-and-white porcelain pagoda in the Philadelphia Hall, produced in China for the Western market, contrasts with the simplicity of the walnut chest labeled by the Quaker cabinetmaker William Savery.

Patuxent Room

Historic items in the Patuxent Room include the embroidered bed hangings owned by the Penn family and Paul Revere's engraving of British troops landing at Boston.

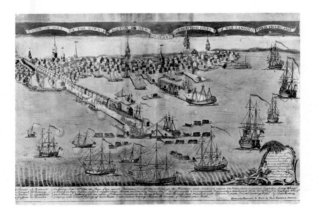

As was customary for American houses of the first half of the eighteenth century, the walls of the Patuxent Room are fully paneled and are here painted a yellow-gray. The room takes its name from the source of the woodwork, Patuxent Manor, a plantation house on the Patuxent River near Lower Marlboro, Maryland, completed about 1744 by Charles Grahame, who had come to Maryland from England two years earlier.

The great mahogany bed, hung with crewel embroidered curtains owned in Pennsylvania by the Penn family, commands the room, which recalls a frequent eighteenth-century practice of using a bedroom as a sitting room. A Philadelphia tea table with a scalloped, or "piecrust," top is set with English porcelain decorated with transfer-printed scenes of a tea party. The leaf-shaped plate, holding spoons made by William Homes, of Boston, is initialed by Robert Hancock, who made the engraved designs for the Worcester factory. The teakettle on a stand is of Continental pewter. At the right is a mahogany chair, probably of Philadelphia origin, its seat covered with pale-green Italian brocatelle; and in the corner a chair from the same set stands beside a Philadelphia dressing table on which is an unusual dressing stand from Massachusetts, its elaborate gilt looking glass frame suspended between spiral-turned posts. A pair of Philadelphia card tables flanks the bed, and above the table on the right is a rare engraving by Paul Revere. Issued in 1770, it is inscribed *A View of Part of the Town of Boston in New-England and Brittish Ships of War Landing Their Troops! 1768* and protests the sending of British regulars to Boston to police the rebellious colonists. Others of a group of important prints in the room hang over the dressing table: a view of Philadelphia, done about 1767 and showing the Pennsylvania Hospital and the Alms House; an engraved portrait of George Washington by John Norman after Benjamin Blyth, published in Boston in 1782; and a mezzotint portrait of John Paul Jones.

An English brass chandelier hangs from the ceiling. Silver candlesticks can be seen on the card tables. The carpet in the foreground is a seventeenth-century Kuba, while small Oriental rugs are at either side of the bed.

Marlboro Room

Among the Philadelphia furniture in the Marlboro Room are four walnut stools made by John Elliott for Charles Norris, whose daughter, Deborah, married George Logan in 1781. The stools then were used at Stenton, the Logan house in Germantown.

Paneling from the entrance floor rooms at Patuxent Manor was combined to form the Marlboro Room. A story and a half in height and built of brick with tall, narrow windows, Patuxent Manor was typical of eighteenth-century houses in Virginia and southern Maryland. The original iron fireback in the fireplace is inscribed POTUXENT 1744. Recalling the aristocratic life lead by Maryland planters is the portrait by Charles Willson Peale of Richard Bennett Lloyd, the handsome younger brother of Edward Lloyd, the "patriot." Wye House, their ancestral home on the Eastern Shore, was destroyed by the British during the Revolution.

The furnishings of the Marlboro Room range in date from the early eighteenth century until about 1800. At the right is a Philadelphia Queen Anne sofa, its cabriole legs ending in carved pad feet. In front of it a walnut candlestand is flanked by Philadelphia corner chairs. Close to the fireplace are two Philadelphia easy chairs displaying a feature almost unique in American furniture: cabriole rear legs matching the shell-carved front legs. Beyond these is a gaming table surrounded by four pad-foot stools dating from about 1756 and made by John Elliott, of Philadelphia. The armchair at the left is the only chair in the full Chippendale style known to bear the label of William Savery. Beyond it is another armchair, transitional in style and also labeled by Savery. The upholstery on the chairs and the sofa is a sand-colored brocatelle, and curtains of dull-gold damask hang at the windows.

Over the fireplace is an important example of American needlework. Still in its original walnut frame and worked by Sarah Warren, of Barnstable, Massachusetts, in 1748, it depicts a scene usually described as "The Fishing Lady on Boston Common." A three-quarter length portrait of George Washington, by Charles Peale Polk, nephew of Charles Willson Peale, hangs between the windows.

The pair of gilded wood-and-tin chandeliers are of the type used in eighteenth-century American ballrooms and churches. Additional light in the room is provided by American iron-and-brass candlestands and imported brass candlesticks and wall sconces. The brass andirons and matching fire tools were probably made in Boston between 1760 and 1775. Almost covering the hard pine floor is a Feraghan carpet, woven in Persia early in the nineteenth century in colors that complement the green paneled walls.

Charleston Dining Room

"Stone," a warm gray color, presumably imitating Portland stone, was frequently mentioned in the advertisements of eighteenth-century paint shops; and the sandy color of the walls, matching the original paint in the Charleston Dining Room, is probably a variation of this oft-mentioned shade. The woodwork is from the large frame house built on Broad Street in Charleston, South Carolina, about 1772 by William Burrows, a lawyer, judge, and landholder. As in many Charleston houses, the main living rooms were on the second floor; and this room is thought to have been the drawing room. In later years the Burrows house became a stylish hotel known as the

Mansion House, and such noted persons as Fanny Kemble and Samuel F. B. Morse stopped there when visiting Charleston. At that time this room was used as a dining room, and it is appropriate that lunch is served here to visitors taking the full-day tour of the Museum. The architectural quality of the room is heightened by pedimented doorways and a dentiled cornice; carved foliage decorates the mantel frieze and the overmantel frame. The bay window at the left originally projected over the entrance porch, which opened onto Broad Street. It now overlooks a small indoor garden simulating the walled gardens of Charleston.

The three-part Massachusetts dining table is set with English pewter plates and Chinese export porcelain. Surrounding the table is a group of twelve walnut chairs, of the simple type of Rhode Island chair with pierced splats and pad feet, thought to have been exported by the Newport cabinetmakers who conducted an extensive "venture" trade with the Southern Colonies and the West Indies. The seats are covered with leather from the Winterthur herd. Newport chairs of a more sophisticated variety, having solid splats and claw-and-ball feet, are at the small trestle table in the bay window.

The interior of the fireplace is lined with white delft tiles customary in Charleston, and a coal-burning grate is used rather than andirons. Over the fireplace is a double portrait attributed to Thomas McIlworth, who worked in New York about 1760. Green silk curtains trimmed with gold fringe hang at the windows, and an English cut-glass chandelier, dating from about 1760, lights the room. Symbolizing the hospitality for which Charleston was noted, a pewter monteith is placed on the marble-topped side table at the right.

In the Charleston Dining Room is a mahogany side table with a top of imported marble. Bought at auction in Charleston a generation ago, it is thought to have been made there.

The Federal Period 1785–1840

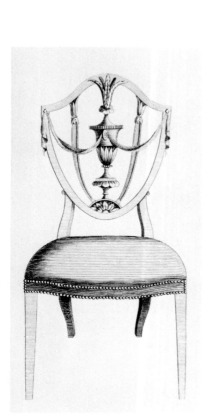

In the years between 1785 and 1840, Americans established the federal form of their government, pushed back the frontier, and expanded their commercial activities to include trade with the Far East. As the citizens of the new Republic spiritually associated themselves with those of ancient Rome, they readily accepted the neo-Roman art forms of the revival that spread through Europe in the second half of the eighteenth century. English and American architectural handbooks popularized the "antique" style which Robert Adam, inspired by the discoveries of Roman art at Pompeii and Herculaneum, had introduced to England in the 1760's. Encouraged by Thomas Jefferson, who patterned his design for the Virginia State Capitol after a Roman temple, Americans built simple and dignified houses embellished with classical details. Ornament, whether carved or molded of plaster, was chosen from the vast vocabulary of classical decoration and patriotic symbols. The American eagle became a favorite device in both architecture and furniture.

English furniture pattern books were imported to America, the most influential being those of George Hepplewhite and Thomas Sheraton. The chair design on this page, taken from Plate 2 of Hepplewhite's *The Cabinet-Maker and Upholsterer's Guide,* was followed by the American craftsman who made the side chair in China Hall (opposite page). The taste expressed in such books endorsed furniture of graceful outline; emphasis was placed on smooth veneered surfaces, often embellished with inlay, delicate carving, or painted decoration. Following or adapting the dictates of the English designers, such American craftsmen as Samuel McIntire, John Seymour, and Duncan Phyfe often supplied their patrons with suites of handsome furniture.

Direct trade with China, begun in 1785, brought into American houses large sets of Chinese export porcelain, frequently made to order with appropriate decorations, monograms, or patterns. Also working in the classical mode, American silversmiths, of whom Paul Revere is the best known, produced tea sets, pitchers, and flatware. Still, Americans depended upon English and European sources for pottery, for brass and silver-plated objects, for wallpapers, carpets, chintzes, and finer textiles. In rooms where plaster walls were painted in soft shades and decoration was largely confined to mantelpieces and the moldings around doors and windows, such treasures helped to "unite elegance and utility," as suggested in the preface to the 1794 edition of Hepplewhite's *Guide.*

China Hall

Plaster ornament, characteristic of the Federal period, is applied to the doorway and window trim from a late-eighteenth-century house in Georgetown, District of Columbia. In the cupboard is part of the blue-bordered Chinese export porcelain dinner service ordered by George Washington in 1785 and bearing the emblem of the Order of the Cincinnati, the hereditary society formed by officers of the Continental Army. The mahogany window seat is attributed to Samuel McIntire, of Salem, Massachusetts, as is the side chair next to it. Gauze curtains embroidered with sequins hang at the window; a Baku carpet is on the floor.

Library Cross Hall

Representative objects of the Federal period in the Library Cross Hall are an English oil lamp based upon the invention of Ami Argand, and a mahogany and satinwood sewing table made in Salem, Massachusetts. Mending and sewing materials were stored in the silk bag suspended from the bottom drawer.

The woodwork in the Library Cross Hall comes from Montmorenci, a house built at Shocco Springs, near Warrenton, North Carolina, about 1822; it preserves the cocoa color of the original paint, offering a foil for the subtle shades in the French wallpaper that covers the walls. Printed in Paris in 1815 by the firm of Joseph Dufour, this scenic design was especially popular in America, where it was advertised in the *New England Palladium* for December 2, 1817, along with other imported papers, by James Foster as "Setts of monuments of Paris, a very elegant Hanging." In this paper the important buildings of Paris are shown as if lined up along the Seine River, and in the foreground are figures in a pastoral setting. Visible at the corner of the Cross Hall are the Pantheon, the Place Vendôme, the Tour St.-Jacques, and the Val-de-Grace.

Among the New England furniture here is a pair of settees with reeded splats, made in Portsmouth, New Hampshire, and attributed to Langley Boardman, who established a shop at 3 Congress Street in Portsmouth before 1800. The green silk upholstery is fastened to the seats with brass tacks in a pattern shown in Plate 4 of Hepplewhite's *Guide*. Between the settees is a mahogany and satinwood sewing table, a form frequently seen in the Federal period. This piece is thought to have been made by Nehemiah Adams, who worked in Salem, Massachusetts, between 1790 and 1840 and whose product is represented by several pieces in the Winterthur collection. A New York side chair stands at the left of one of the settees, its seat covered in similar green silk. Beyond it, New England card tables flank a sofa characteristic of Salem, with turned arm supports and a veneered cresting, and covered with a pink and green striped silk material. On the card tables are Argand lamps, silver plated and incorporating the principle developed in 1783 by Ami Argand, a Swiss physicist, to increase the brilliance of an oil lamp by means of a cylindrical wick. The oil drained from the urn-shaped drum to the wick, which burned by means of a central updraft of air. Similar units are in the pair of lamps hanging from the ceiling. Strongly colored nineteenth-century Joshaghan runners on the floor contrast with the soft colors of the furniture and wallpaper. The door in the background leads to the Montmorenci Stair Hall, where the woodwork is also from Montmorenci, at Shocco Springs, North Carolina.

Salem Stair Hall

A stairway from an eighteenth-century house in Salem, Massachusetts, provides the setting for a sofa attributed to the Salem carver Samuel McIntire. Above the sofa is a painting of Canton, one of a set brought to Philadelphia about 1819. Beyond the arch, a card table and side chair probably made in Duncan Phyfe's shop, stand beneath a gilt looking glass, also from New York. French rugs grace the floor.

Vickers Alcove

Wallpaper dating from about 1795 frames the doorway of the Vickers Alcove, where a hanging shelf holds a unique group of decorated porcelain plates and dishes made in 1824 and signed by John Vickers, who operated a pottery in Uwchland Township, Chester County, Pennsylvania, between 1822 and 1860. The furniture here includes a sewing table attributed to John Seymour; a cylinder-top desk considered to be the work of William Hook, of Salem, Massachusetts; and a Philadelphia side chair. The porcelain for which the room is named predates that made in the Philadelphia factory of William Ellis Tucker.

Dining Room Cross Hall

A Palladian window and Ionic pilasters from Port Royal, built at Frankford, Pennsylvania, in 1762, provide architectural interest in the Dining Room Cross Hall; and important Massachusetts furniture of the Federal period is displayed in this setting. At the left is a mahogany desk and bookcase made in Salem by Nehemiah Adams and shipped to Capetown, South Africa, an item in the "venture cargo" trade frequently engaged in by New England cabinetmakers. In the bookcase section is part of a French porcelain dessert service ordered by President James Monroe. A chair in front of the desk and matching ones flanking it are attributed to the Salem carver Samuel McIntire and are like chairs made for Elias Hasket Derby, the merchant

Silver trinkets once presented to Indian chiefs include medals and an arm band, by Joseph Richardson, Jr., similar to one shown in Saint-Mémin's water-color portrait of an Osage warrior.

prince of Salem. In the foreground is a chair of similar design taken from Hepplewhite's *Guide,* but presumably made in Philadelphia, where Derby purchased a large set of painted chairs in 1796. Beside it is a half-round pier table of mahogany and maple with applied ornament, probably made in Boston and showing a closer relationship to the designs of Robert Adam than most American furniture.

Beyond the archway is a sofa thought to have been made by Nehemiah Adams and carved by McIntire. It is upholstered in accordance with instructions in Sheraton's *Cabinet-Maker's and Upholsterer's Drawing-Book.* The carving on the pair of chairs in front of it is also attributed to McIntire, as is that on the sofa beneath the window. At the left of this sofa is a writing desk, one of the few pieces labeled by John Seymour, of Boston. On its writing surface are silver medals given as tokens of good will to Indian chiefs by the President of the United States. An upholstered armchair by Stephen Badlam, of Dorchester, Massachusetts, stands beside the desk.

Cut-glass wall sconces provide light in the hall, as does an oil lamp with a base of Wedgwood jasper ware. Prints of naval battles of the War of 1812 hang on the wall, and over the Adams sofa is a water-color portrait of an Osage warrior, painted by the French émigré Saint-Mémin in Washington in 1804. The carpets are Persian.

Montmorenci Stair Hall

The graceful free-hanging staircase dominating the Montmorenci Stair Hall was formerly the outstanding feature of Montmorenci, a famous house built at Shocco Springs, near Warrenton, North Carolina, about 1822 by General William Williams. Lafayette, on his tour of the United States in 1824 to 1825, was entertained at Montmorenci, and here a later owner's daughter, Lucy Williams, was married to the brother of President James Knox Polk. The staircase was probably made by a North Carolina craftsman, but whether it was designed by a professional architect is not known. It resembles the design for an "elliptical stairs" illustrated in Peter Nicholson's *The Carpenter's New Guide,* a builder's handbook first published in London in 1792 and widely used in America during the first half of the nineteenth century. Gouge carving and finely molded plasterwork, probably made in Philadelphia and bearing a resemblance to the work of Robert Wellford, reflect the refined taste of the Federal period.

Augmenting the architectural splendor is furniture by skilled craftsmen of the early Republic. The mahogany and satinwood chairs and settees, upholstered in old green silk, represent the product of John Seymour and his son Thomas, who worked in Boston from 1796 into the early years of the nineteenth century. The octagonal sewing table between the side chairs is a further example of the Seymours' furniture, which is unmatched for its delicacy of form and exquisitely detailed inlay. Also in the room, and illustrative of the French influence on American decorative art at this time, is a mahogany and satinwood pier table, bearing the label of Charles Honoré Lannuier, a French émigré cabinetmaker who worked at 60 Broad Street, New York, from 1805 until 1819. Looking glasses, gilded and embellished with delicate foliage motifs popular in the Federal period, reflect the light of candles held in late-eighteenth-century candelabra and sconces of cut glass.

Chinese export porcelain, imported in quantities in American ships, is represented by punch bowls on the side tables and pistol-handled urns elsewhere in the room. A portrait of Catherine Browne, of New York, sometimes called the "tragic Kate Browne," hangs above the settee. On the floor are Persian Feraghan carpets dating from the early nineteenth century. The spindles of the stair railing and the soft moldings of the plaster cornice cast numerous shadows around the room. Mahogany paneled doors from Montmorenci contrast with the ivory-colored walls.

In the Montmorenci Stair Hall are porcelain punch
bowls and ornamental urns (facing page) made in China
for export to the West. Among them is a pistol-
handled urn patterned after a model first executed
at the Marieberg factory in Sweden and representative
of many made for the American market.

McIntire Bedroom

*Reflecting the patriotism of nineteenth-century
Americans are such items in the McIntire Bedroom as
Staffordshire jugs bearing portraits of Commodore
Bainbridge and Captain Jacob Jones, heroes of the
War of 1812, and a gilt bronze clock inscribed
WASHINGTON, First in WAR, First in PEACE,
First in the HEARTS of his COUNTRYMEN.*

So named to honor Samuel McIntire, one of the best known of American craftsmen, is the McIntire Bedroom. McIntire was born in Salem, Massachusetts, in 1757 and was trained as a housewright, but is remembered as an architect and carver. While no furniture is known to have been made by him, he did carve for other craftsmen; and many skillfully decorated pieces of furniture are attributed to his hand, among them several in this room. The woodwork here is from the Philadelphia town house built in 1812 by Robert Wellford and later owned by Peter Breen, a distiller. The plaster decoration on the mantel, featuring a scene of the Battle of Lake Erie, was probably made at Wellford's American Manufactory of Composition Ornaments on South Tenth Street, not far from the house. Painted a dove gray, the woodwork is in striking contrast to the yellow satin on the chairs in the room.

In front of the fireplace is a pair of upholstered armchairs, their carved crestings containing elements characteristic of McIntire's work. Facing them is an armchair, one of a set McIntire finished for Jarathmeel Peirce, of Salem, in 1802. Its design is based on a "parlour chair" shown on Plate 33 of Sheraton's *Drawing-Book*. A pair of side chairs made in Salem flanks a mahogany dressing table, also from Salem, above which hangs a Philadelphia looking glass ornamented with a view of the Battle of Lake Erie. At the right of the bed is a small marble-topped table with a tambour door, attributed to the shop of John Seymour. The bed complements the Philadelphia woodwork, for it was made in 1796 by Jacob Wayne of that city. It is hung with curtains of a rich gold brocatelle, and at its foot is a kidney-shaped sewing table of satinwood and thought to be from the shop of Ephraim Haines, also a leading cabinetmaker in Philadelphia.

In the archway leading to the hall is a cupboard filled with Staffordshire jugs commemorating events in the War of 1812, and on the mantelshelf is a French clock eulogizing George Washington. Above it hangs a painting of the view from Belmont, an eighteenth-century mansion overlooking Philadelphia. The gold, brown, and purple shades of the French tapestry-weave rug unify the various colors and textures in the room.

Sheraton Room

A green Venetian blind hangs at the window of the Sheraton Room, where the woodwork is from Mordington, built near Frederica, Delaware, in 1785. Walls of shell pink set off the green silk gauze canopy on the bed. With the exception of the high-backed upholstered chair from Philadelphia, the furniture here is of New England origin, including the unusual Massachusetts armchair at the secretary desk. The wall clock is a rare example of the work of Aaron Willard. A side chair possibly made by John Seymour stands next to a bow-front chest. The rug is a Bokhara.

Winterthur Bedroom

The woodwork in the Winterthur Bedroom is from the section of the house built in 1839. Displayed against pale-blue walls is furniture of the early nineteenth century. A net canopy covers the top of the New England field bed. At the right are painted chairs usually described as "fancy Sheraton," and a stool of this style stands at a table holding an American embroidery frame. The unusual wall clock is attributed to Benjamin Gilman, of Exeter, New Hampshire. A view of St. Paul's Church, New York, hangs above the serpentine chest of drawers. The Scotch carpet dates between 1800 and 1820.

Portsmouth Room

The Portsmouth Room contains needlework executed by the distaff members of prominent American families, among them a knitted silk pincushion made by Mary Wright Alsop, of Middletown, Connecticut, and a needlework picture by Sarah Derby, of Salem, Massachusetts, with the faces of the figures painted, according to tradition, by John Singleton Copley.

The Portsmouth Room has woodwork from an early-nineteenth-century house in Portsmouth, New Hampshire; furniture from northern New England; and many examples of the handiwork of early American women. Dominating the room is a large needlework picture based upon an engraving by Jean Le Pautre and worked with silk threads in the 1760's by Sarah, daughter of Captain Richard Derby, of Salem, Massachusetts. It is flanked by two early-nineteenth-century pictures symbolizing the continents of America and Europe, done with silk and wool threads on a painted silk background. Above a maple worktable from New England is a needlework landscape. The glass of the original frame is lettered A VIEW OF NEW YORK BY MARY BOWEN. IN. THE. 10th YEAR OF HER AGE 1807. On the table top are scissors, steel knitting needles, and a steel bobbin. The brass double candlestick with a green shade is of French origin.

The practice of hooking rugs of wool or cotton in brightly colored patterns imitative of Aubusson carpets was widespread in New England. The unusually brilliant rugs here—almost a pair—were made in the nineteenth century, probably at Waldoboro, Maine, where many fine hooked rugs were produced.

Arranged in the room is painted furniture made in Boston or Salem. The black-painted settee and armchairs are grouped around a graceful sewing table, made about 1810 and signed by Vose and Coats, of Boston. Its maple surface is decorated with paintings of sea shells. The side chairs flanking the settee are ornamented with gilt trophies of musical instruments. All have seat cushions covered in French painted silk of the late eighteenth century. At the right is a red-and-gold "fancy" chair from New York State, its rush seat painted in red and white stripes. Also from New York is the white-painted armchair at the left of the door. In front of the small easy chair covered in green taffeta is a decorated maple sewing table; above it is an American wall clock with elaborate stenciled gilt decoration. The frosted glass bowl of the hanging lamp, made toward the middle of the nineteenth century, is embellished with painted flowers. The walls of the room are a light green, and the woodwork a deep ivory.

Architect's Room

In the eighteenth century in both England and America, a knowledge of architecture was considered essential to a gentleman's education. In recognition of this cultural fact, the Architect's Room is arranged to display books, instruments, and other accouterments of the gentlemanly practice of architecture. The Palladian window, virtually a symbol of academic architecture in the eighteenth century, is of a type often seen in Connecticut, where other woodwork in the room originated. White walls and off-white trim provide a setting for mahogany furniture of the Federal period.

English brass oil lamps employing the principle of Ami Argand are on the window sill. A drafting table, made between 1810 and 1820 and labeled by Thomas Needham, of Salem, Massachusetts, stands in front of the window. On its raised working surface, whale-oil lamps light drafting instruments of various sorts and documents pertaining to building, among them an 1812 letter from the Postmaster General detailing the expenses of finishing Blodget's Hotel in Washington, and a report from William Lee, "agent for procuring furniture for President's House," describing the furnishing of the White House for President Monroe in 1819. New England painted chairs with rush seats stand at either side of the desk. The other chairs in the room are of New York origin and feature carved urn-shaped splats derived from Plate 41 of Sheraton's *Drawing-Book*. An architectural rendering of a pedimented mantelpiece inscribed *Chimney Breast for the Dining Room, 18 Jany, 1770* rests on the mahogany reading stand in the corner; and books on architecture, science, and other intellectual pursuits fill the shelves of the mahogany break-front bookcase made in Massachusetts about 1795. The silver inkstand in the desk compartment was made in London in 1823. A water color by John Thomas Serres, depicting the battle between the *Reindeer* and the *Wasp* during the War of 1812, hangs on the wall. Inscribed *The Wasp with her gib boom in the Reindeer's lee rigging,* the painting by this English artist is one of a set of four in the room.

The late-eighteenth-century brass chandelier is of English origin, and wall sconces with glass shades provide additional light. The rug is a tapestry weave, probably made in France in the early years of the nineteenth century, and features flowers against a deep-brown background. Through the window is a view of the woodland that surrounds Winterthur.

*Among the drafting equipment displayed in the
Architect's Room is a shagreen case containing in fitted
compartments a drawing pen, dividers, a brass
protractor, and ivory rules—all of English origin.
The cover, lined with paper, is inscribed in ink with
the name of a previous owner, J. S. Hollaway.*

Franklin Room

Franklin commemorative objects in the Franklin Room include a nineteenth-century paperweight with a sulphide bust of Franklin, possibly of American origin; a Wedgwood and Bentley jasper-ware plaque after the portrait done in 1777 by Jean Baptiste Nini; and a Staffordshire figure made in the nineteenth century and incorrectly labeled Washington.

Even during his lifetime, the prestige of Benjamin Franklin was world wide: His experiments in electricity accorded him a status comparable to that of Isaac Newton; his achievements in diplomacy played a major part in the successful conclusion of the American Revolution; and his advice at the Constitutional Convention helped to shape the new nation. Admiring Europeans and Americans preserved the image of Franklin in numerous ways, and in the Franklin Room are a number of objects decorated with his portrait. The marble fireplace in the room, from a house in Charlestown, Massachusetts, is carved with Franklin's bust. At one season of the year an English printed cotton, generally known as the *Apotheosis of Franklin,* is used for bed hangings and window curtains. Franklin's writings lie on the table; his portrait hangs on the wall; pottery figures record his appearance.

The furniture here is from different parts of the country. The Massachusetts bed is similar to one in the Pingree house in Salem, Massachusetts. Its unusual carved and painted canopy features a device of Cupid's bow and quiver, and the torch of Hymen; embroidered cotton draperies hang from it. Beside the bed a figure of Benjamin Franklin stands on a marble-topped oval night stand with a tambour door. A New York washstand is in the corner, and beside it, an armchair from Salem or Boston, its design adapted from a plate in Hepplewhite's *Guide.* Between the windows is a sofa, upholstered in eighteenth-century French silk brocade. It belonged originally to Victor Marie du Pont, who lived in New York until 1805 and used it in his house on Liberty Street. Above the sofa hangs a gold-and-white looking glass, neoclassical in outline and topped by a gilded eagle finial, a popular decoration in the Federal period. Franklin's books, a paperweight, and a silver-plated oil lamp are on the New York drum table. The mahogany armchair at the left is of Philadelphia origin.

A Khorassan rug of the early nineteenth century is on the floor. Red-and-white English printed cotton curtains hang at the windows, offset by light-blue walls and ivory-colored woodwork.

Somerset Room

Jerathmael Bowers was born in Somerset (then part of Swansea) on the Taunton River in Massachusetts, and followed in the footsteps of his father as a shipbuilder and merchant. In 1763 he married Mary Sherburne, an heiress from Boston; and at about that time he built, on a tract called *Labour in Vain,* a large wooden house, the dining room of which contained the unusual paneling in the Somerset Room. The house was inherited in 1799 by his son, John, whose charming personality and elegant, but extravagant, manner of living is legendary in Somerset; and presumably the woodwork in the dining room was modernized at that time. Neoclassical details in the mantelpiece, based upon designs in William Pain's *Practical Builder,* which was published in an

American edition in Boston in 1792, and the applied moldings on the doors and dado indicate the renovation. Original sandstone slabs form the sides of the fireplace, which is framed by gray marble. An unusual color scheme is followed, preserving the original: The woodwork is moss green; the walls, a pale blue-green; and the ceilings of the arches, sky blue.

Against this background is furniture of Massachusetts origin, representative of both the Chippendale and Federal periods. The settee at the left, an unusual double-chair-back form, is an impressive example of the Massachusetts Chippendale style. Beside it is a tilt-top oval stand labeled by Joseph Short, who worked in Newburyport, Massachusetts, between 1792 and 1819. A straight-legged Massachusetts armchair with a pierced splat stands at the right of the fireplace; and next to it is a side chair with upholstered seat and carved slats, a type generally called *ladder back* and thought to have been made in Massachusetts toward the end of the eighteenth century. A pair of Philadelphia ladder-back chairs, whose tapered legs suggest the new style of the Federal period, flanks a mahogany drop-leaf breakfast table made by Elijah and Jacob Sanderson, of Salem, Massachusetts. Above the table is a needlework hatchment done in silk and metal threads and inscribed *By the Name of Jackson,* and at either side of it are unusual double-branched sconces with scalloped wooden backplates painted green.

German porcelain ice pails produced about 1800 stand on the breakfast table, and English porcelain figures attributed to the Bow or Derby factory adorn the mantelshelf. On the floor is a Turkish carpet of the early nineteenth century.

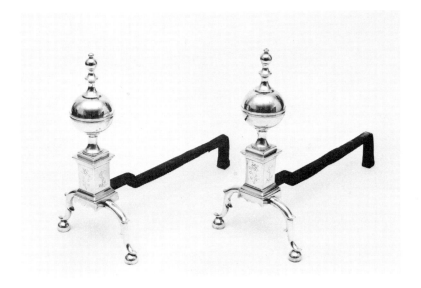

In the fireplace of the Somerset Room are brass andirons attributed to Richard Whittingham, of New York, and a cast-iron fireback (above) dated 1781 and inscribed SOLD BY JOSEPH WEBB, BOSTON.

Counting Room

Merchants of the eighteenth and nineteenth centuries often had their offices in their homes, and the domestic atmosphere of such places of business might be suggested by the Counting Room. Here, the woodwork, including the stair railing, is from the Red Lion Inn, built about 1800 at Red Lion, Delaware. The plaster walls are a deep-buff color, and the trim, a blue-gray.

Under the oval window in the recess is a mahogany desk that descended in the family of a Marblehead, Massachusetts, sea captain. The brass drawer pulls and the inlaid patera of satinwood, a customary neoclassical decoration, repeat the shape of the window. English copper candlesticks, an eighteenth-century hourglass, and an inkstand sold by Boughman, Thomas and Company, of Wilmington, Delaware, rest on the top of the desk. Beside it, a tall stool from New England, painted green, stands under hanging pine shelves which hold ledgers and account books, as well as white pottery eagles attributed to the Phoenixville factory; an octagonal ivory bird cage once owned in Duxbury, Massachusetts; and a fishing kit, which includes maps of the original owner's favorite fishing spots. The spittoon under the desk was made at the Eagle Porcelain Works in Lancaster, Pennsylvania.

Above the stairway is a nineteenth-century model of a three-masted American ship of the line. Beneath it hangs a banner presumably carried in one of the parades that characterized the temperance movement of the nineteenth century. Chairs made in Connecticut or Rhode Island about 1790 stand against the railing; between them is a New England maple candlestand. On a walnut table in the foreground, a mahogany liquor chest holds square glass bottles decorated with gilt designs. A brightly colored hooked rug covers the floor.

An American iron chandelier hangs from the ceiling; an eighteenth-century iron candlestand stands beside the desk; and on top of the shelves is a tin oil lamp. Among the books in the shelves are such pertinent titles as *The Merchant's Magazine, The Pocket Companion; or, Every Man his Own Lawyer,* and *The American Ship-Master's Guide and Commercial Assistant.*

Among the many objects in the Counting Room are a hanging pipe box originally owned in Nantucket and a nineteenth-century fishing kit that belonged to John Weidman, of Union Forge, Pennsylvania.

Federal Parlor

The Federal Parlor, formerly one of the handsome rooms in the Phelps-Hatheway house at Suffield, Connecticut, exhibits the elegance of a prosperous New Englander's home in the 1790's. In 1788, the same year in which he acquired title to the vast Genesee tract in New York State, Oliver Phelps purchased the Burbank house in Suffield; and six years later he began to remodel it in a style compatible with the large fortune he was amassing in land speculations in western New York and Ohio. In this house Phelps placed impressive neoclassical woodwork enriched with plaster composition ornament and complemented it with French wallpapers in the "Etruscan style," reflecting the influence of Robert Adam upon the designers of French papers. The soft beige color of the woodwork is offset by the terra-cotta border on the ceiling, one of the few American examples of an ornamented ceiling, and by the predominantly blue tones of the wallpaper which bears a stamp believed to be that of Réveillon, dating from about 1790 and probably part of the paper purchased for Phelps in Boston.

Oliver Phelps patronized local craftsmen, bought furniture in New York, and imported decorative objects from France; these facts are reflected by the furnishings of the room. The cherry desk and bookcase, featuring an unusual pierced pediment and doors inlaid with representations of the American eagle, was made in the Connecticut Valley and has been attributed to Eliphalet Chapin, of East Windsor; the cherry shield-back chair in front of it is also from Connecticut. A Connecticut upholstered armchair, popularly called a *Martha Washington chair* and covered in yellow and gray striped silk, stands at the left of the fireplace. Also from New England is a pair of side chairs, or back stools, upholstered in light-blue moiré silk. The benches in the window recesses, found in Salem, Massachusetts, display original black paint with gilt decoration. A New England sewing table stands in the corner at the left, and on a Connecticut candlestand beside the fireplace is an English enameled coffee urn, its silver rim bearing the date letter of 1802–1803. English luster figures decorate the mantelshelf, and Chinese export porcelain cups are seen on the Connecticut cherry table at the left. Draperies fashioned of red silk twill lined with green taffeta are hung at the windows in a manner characteristic of the Federal period. American brass andirons and fire tools are used in the fireplace. On the floor is a nineteenth-century Persian carpet.

On the writing surface of the desk and bookcase in
the Federal Parlor is a watch sold by Abraham Stein,
who had a shop at 86 North Third Street, Philadelphia,
between 1795 and 1825. The enameled calendar dial
is decorated with miniature landscapes typical of the
neoclassical taste.

Carroll Stair Hall

Perhaps inspired by the paintings of the Hudson River School, or more directly by the scenery of nearby Lake Otsego, William Price, the itinerant artist who painted the walls of the Carroll Stair Hall, then in a house at East Springfield, New York, combined ivy-covered ruins, palm trees encircled by vines, and steamboats in a panorama of a mountainous landscape.

The Carroll Stair Hall, from the Carroll house at East Springfield, New York, is a dramatic example of nineteenth-century American wall decoration. Both levels of the hall are here installed, a project which involved bracing (between cardboard panels) sections of the plaster on the original lath and studs, transporting them to Winterthur, and reassembling the walls in the Museum. Additional wall paintings from the Carroll house are displayed at the Farmers' Museum in Cooperstown, New York.

That French wallpapers such as those in the Federal Parlor (page 103) and the Library Cross Hall (page 81) were popular in this country is evidenced by frequent references in newspaper advertisements, and it is to be expected that those unable to have imported papers would attempt the same effect with freehand paintings. This was done for Ezra Carroll, who had moved to Springfield from Connecticut in 1814 and who was one of many New Englanders who went westward as the lands in New York State were opened for settlement. His house in Springfield was of the traditional New England form, with rooms on either side of a center hall; and all the rooms were decorated in a whimsical, if somewhat bizarre, manner by William Price, who painted with oil colors directly on the plaster, signing his name and the date *1831* on the wall at the top of the stairs to record these paintings as his only known work. Obviously Price was inspired by contemporary wallpapers; but with a vivid imagination he created in the Carroll house a romantic landscape of waterfalls, rivers, and hills, and included in it such unlikely elements as classical ruins, steamboats, plantation houses, oversized fruit trees, and stylishly dressed ladies and gentlemen.

Another native interpretation of French design is represented by New England hooked rugs in bright colors which complement those of the oil paintings. At the left is a "fancy Sheraton" chair, probably made by William Buttre, of Albany, who advertised and illustrated chairs of this type in 1815. A cherry handrail and balusters offset the apple-green color of the stairs and woodwork.

Winterthur Hall

An English hall lamp and gilded metal sconces light a section of the Winterthur Hall, which preserves woodwork from the original part of Winterthur, built in 1839. Above a mahogany serving table labeled by Mark Pitman, of Salem, Massachusetts, hangs a still-life painting inscribed on the back: *Painted by James Peale in the 79th year of his Age 1828*. Shield-back side chairs, made in New York between 1790 and 1800, stand beside the table; and on top of it is a Chinese export porcelain bowl decorated with symbols of the Masonic Order. The carpet is a nineteenth-century Kabistan.

Gold and White Room

Displayed against pale-green walls in the Gold and White Room is furniture painted white with gilt decoration. The bed, side chair, and settee shown here were once owned by Governor Joseph C. Yates of New York. The dressing table at the right, also painted white, is from Massachusetts, as is the upholstered armchair standing next to a satinwood table made in the Louis XVI style by Charles Honoré Lannuier, of New York. On the wall is a presentation timepiece by Simon Willard. The colors of the English needlework rug complement the green silk bedspread and window curtains.

Du Pont Dining Room

In the years immediately following the Revolution there were close political ties between the United States and France, and in the Du Pont Dining Room there are suggestions of French decorative styles as well. Dominating the room is a tapestry-weave carpet in shades of tan and red, inscribed with the legend: *Man^re Royale d'Aubusson 1767*. Hanging at the window are blue lampas curtains woven in France from designs by Phillippe de Lassalle, court textile designer to Louis XVI.

Hanging above the eight-legged New York sideboard is one of the important paintings in the Winterthur collection. Begun in 1782 by Benjamin West, it is a sketch for a commemorative picture of the commissioners meeting in Paris to negotiate the peace treaty between England and the American states. Shown in the picture are John Jay, John Adams, Henry Laurens, Benjamin Franklin, and his grandson William Temple Franklin. Portraits of the British commissioners were never included. On the sideboard are urn-shaped knife cases once owned by Elias Hasket Derby and a set of six silver tankards made by the Boston patriot and silversmith, Paul Revere, and given by the widow of Ephraim Bartlett to the First Church in Brookfield, Massachusetts, in 1768.

The three-part mahogany dining table was made in Baltimore and is embellished with inlaid devices of the American eagle taken from the great seal of the United States, which had been adopted by Congress in 1782. The table is set for dessert, without a cloth, in accordance with eighteenth-century custom. Silver-luster figures form part of the centerpiece, along with English silver candlesticks matching those on the sideboard. Blown-glass wine bottles are set out, and at each place are Chinese export porcelain plates. Around the table are mahogany chairs from a set made in New York for Victor Marie du Pont, who lived there until 1805.

Chinese porcelain is also shown behind the glazed doors of the New England break-front secretary. On the Baltimore bottle chest in the corner is a silver pitcher made by Paul Revere in the shape of a Staffordshire jug, and on the swell-front sideboard of New England origin are New England silver tankards and a glass punch bowl engraved with the seal of the Society of the Cincinnati. A mahogany-and-gilt looking glass with a scrolled pediment hangs against the cream-colored paneled wall, which comes from Readbourne, built about 1733 at Centreville, Maryland.

On the sideboard in the Du Pont Dining Room is a mahogany knife case; above it hangs Benjamin West's sketch of the Americans who negotiated peace with Great Britain in 1782.

Nemours Room

When Pierre Samuel du Pont served in the French National Assembly, he adopted the identifying suffix *Nemours,* the name of the district he represented; and thus *Du Pont de Nemours* originated as the name of the American branch of the family. The Nemours Room contains a number of family mementos, including, at one season of the year, a silk lampas bedspread which has descended in the family.

Retaining its original cocoa color, carved and reeded woodwork from the dining room of Montmorenci at Shocco Springs, North Carolina, has been installed here; and the plaster walls are painted a soft shade of green. A garniture of Chinese export porcelain, decorated in sepia and gold, contrasts with the color of the woodwork beneath John Trumbull's portrait of his beautiful English wife, Sarah Hope Harvey, painted about the time of their return to New York in 1804. The brass andirons in the fireplace are of American origin; a pierced brass fender with an eagle design is seen against the white marble hearth.

The velvet-covered armchair, a form much like the French *fauteuil de bureau* and unusual in American furniture, is similar to the work of Henry Connelly, a Philadelphia cabinetmaker prominent in the first quarter of the nineteenth century. The small sofa, upholstered in matching velvet, was probably made in Salem, Massachusetts. A New York armchair made about 1810 is drawn toward a writing table labeled by Michael Allison, of New York; on top of the table are silver spoons made by Henry J. Pepper, of Wilmington, for Eleuthère Irénée du Pont and a silver child's mug used by his grandson Henry Algernon du Pont, born in 1838. On the wall are framed documents, including the identity card E.I. du Pont used in Paris during the Directory, a citation given Pierre Samuel du Pont for his actions as a commander of the National Guard in defense of the King on August 10, 1792, and a pass admitting "Citizen du Pont" to the Tuilleries. The subtle colors of an Aubusson carpet complement the walls and woodwork.

Phyfe Room

In the Phyfe Room, furniture by the New York cabinet-maker Duncan Phyfe illustrates the elegant simplicity of the Federal period. Phyfe, who produced furniture of such grace and quality that his name is one of the most famous in the annals of American craftsmanship, supplied the leading citizens of early-nineteenth-century New York. Among them was William Bayard, who moved to No. 6 State Street, facing Battery Park, in 1806, and to whom Phyfe rendered a bill the following year for some fifty pieces of furniture. Included in the bill were the ten side chairs and two arm-chairs in this room. Just a year before Phyfe made the

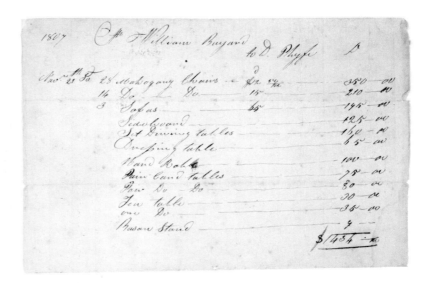

Of particular interest in the *Phyfe Room* is the invoice Duncan Phyfe rendered William Bayard in 1807 for furniture in the room. One of the mahogany chairs described in the bill and listed at $12.50 is shown below.

Bayard furniture, Moses Rogers had remodeled at No. 7 State Street the house that contained the delicately modeled woodwork which here is painted white in contrast to the yellow walls.

The Bayard chairs and the matching window seat are typical of Phyfe's best period of work. Similar to them in form and detail, the caned settee features reeded arms, seat rails, and legs, as well as carved cresting rails. The upholstery on the chairs and settee is a blue-and-yellow lampas, an early-nineteenth-century French material matching that of the curtains, which are fashioned like those in a house on Waverly Place, New York, for which Phyfe supplied all the furniture in 1816.

In front of the caned settee is a sofa table, described by Sheraton as used by ladies "to draw, write, or read upon"; and at either side is a globe stand carved in the manner of Phyfe. Between the windows are tripod-base card tables designed so that two of the feet swing back to balance the table when the folding leaf is opened. The piano at the end of the room bears the patent of John Geib, Jr., for whom Phyfe made several cases; and above it hangs a gilt looking glass ornamented with a panel of eglomisé, or reverse-painted glass. On the right of the looking glass is a portrait of Mrs. Ferdinand Bauduy, nee Victorine du Pont, for whom Phyfe made a sewing table; balancing it is James Frothingham's portrait of Mrs. Simeon Chase Whittier.

Light is provided by silver-plated Argand lamps and cut-glass chandeliers and wall sconces designed in the neoclassic style. The carpet is an Aubusson weave with repeated medallions of flowers against a brown background.

Blue Room

A white dove framed in a blue medallion at the center of an eighteenth-century Savonnerie carpet keys the color scheme of the Blue Room, where the theme is carried out in the mantelpiece, in Wedgwood lamps and candlesticks, and in the color of the walls and upholstery. The mantelpiece, decorated with plaster composition ornaments incorporating busts of George Washington and Benjamin Franklin surrounded by garlands against a blue ground, comes from the Wilson house, built in Salem, New Jersey, about 1810. The fireplace opening is plastered, following a practice common in South Jersey, and contains brass andirons of a type often found in Baltimore.

A small sofa stands at the right of the fireplace. Upholstered in blue and cream striped silk brocade, it is Chippendale in form, but shows the tapered legs of the Federal period. Another form characteristic of this period is the oval-topped mahogany stand in front of the sofa. Matching fire screens, holding silk needlework pictures in oval frames and probably of Massachusetts origin, flank the fireplace. A barrel-shaped easy chair, covered with blue and white striped satin, is at the left. Beside it stands a Philadelphia sewing table of the oval shape occasionally referred to as a *Martha Washington*. Shield-back Philadelphia side chairs dating from about 1790 stand in the window recesses, their dark mahogany frames repeating the tone of the veneered and inlaid pelmets from which the cream-colored silk window valences are suspended. Between the windows is a mahogany and satinwood secretary desk thought to have been made in Philadelphia or Baltimore. Its design is based on a "cabinet" shown in Thomas Sheraton's *Drawing-Book*. Blue-and-white Wedgwood candlesticks light its writing compartment; books, as well as Chinese export porcelain, fill the shelves between the mirrored doors. At the right is the mahogany foot post of a Charleston bed decorated with carved sheaves of rice, a typical ornament on South Carolina furniture.

On the mantelshelf are brass oil lamps with Wedgwood jasper-ware bases, and between them is a group of Staffordshire pottery animals. Above them hangs a silk needlework picture commemorating the Revolutionary heroes Warren, Montgomery, Wooster, and Mercer. It was framed in New York about 1815.

On the mantel in the Blue Room is a pair of lamps
of the type described in English catalogues of the early
nineteenth century as "sideboard lamps." Employing
the Argand principle, the oil was held in cut-glass
receptacles; the bases were ornamented with blue-and-
white Wedgwood sleeves.

Gray Room

In the Gray Room is an oil painting on glass depicting John Paul Jones, soldier of fortune and hero of the Revolution, standing on the deck of his ship. Also in the room is his spyglass, given a number of years later to Samuel Francis du Pont.

Mid-eighteenth-century paneling lines one wall of the Gray Room, where furniture of the early part of the century is combined with small decorative objects dating from about 1800. The rich greenish-gray color of the walls, which gives the room its name, contrasts with the dark-green mantelshelf and the molding around the fireplace. Framing the opening are eighteenth-century purple Delft tiles depicting Biblical scenes, among them *Jonah and the Whale, Tobias and the Angel,* and the *Parable of the Good Samaritan.* Yellow silk bourette curtains hang at the window; their color is repeated in the yellow ground of the Kilim rug, a primitive tapestry weave made in Eastern Europe about 1800.

The blue-painted Queen Anne day bed has a history of ownership in Coatesville, Pennsylvania, and possibly was made in that rural part of

Chester County, forty miles west of Philadelphia. It is covered with a yellow linsey-woolsey quilt. Behind the day bed stands a William and Mary desk-on-frame, painted gray-green; in its writing compartment are an eighteenth-century hourglass and a patent for 130 acres of land in Lancaster County granted to David Livingston by the Penn heirs in 1741. Also on the desk is a stoneware ink well impressed with the signature *C Crolius Manufacturer, Manhattan-Wells, New-York.* Clarkson Crolius operated a pottery at that site from 1800 until 1814. An early-eighteenth-century Pennsylvania armchair in front of the window displays the rush seat and shaped slats of a form which persisted throughout the century.

American wrought-iron andirons with brass finials hold the logs in the fireplace; the fire tools have matching finials. On the square bricks of the hearth is a group of miniature copper teakettles. The bellows leaning against the fireplace jamb is painted white with chinoiserie decoration. A walnut shelf clock, its brass dial inscribed *Willard, Roxbury Street,* is centered between late-eighteenth-century English brass candlesticks.

The chandelier is of American origin, and the mirrored sconce over the desk is an early-nineteenth-century device to increase the effect of candle-light with faceted reflecting surfaces in the backplate. A portrait painted on the reverse side of the glass is entitled *Paul Jones* and depicts the Revolutionary naval hero standing on the deck of his ship. In the opposite corner is John Paul Jones' spyglass, presented in 1851 to Samuel Francis du Pont as a token, according to the inscription on the shaft, of the "high estimation of Capt. Du Pont's public services and private virtues." Samuel Francis du Pont, for whom Du Pont Circle in Washington is named, was the son of Victor Marie du Pont and lived at Louviers, a few miles across the valley from Winterthur.

Red Lion Entrance Hall

The Red Lion Entrance Hall, from the inn at Red Lion, Delaware, is arranged to suggest the spirit of an early-nineteenth-century tavern. Pewter mugs are on the octagonal pine table in the center of the room, and painted Windsor chairs are drawn up to it. Against the wall is a paneled settle; on the shelves at the right and on the Pennsylvania chest beneath them is a collection of painted tin coffeepots and trays of the type often sold by peddlers. Primitive paintings hang on the wall, two depicting incidents in the American Revolution, and the other, Penn's treaty with the Indians. Tin lanterns hang from the ceiling. An oval hooked rug is on the floor.

Commons Room

The woodwork and stairway in the Commons Room also come from the Red Lion Inn, and the furniture displayed here includes a wide variety of Windsor chair forms. An unusual triple-arch settee from Connecticut is flanked by matching low-backed armchairs, probably of Pennsylvania origin. In the background is a comb-back Windsor armchair, also from Pennsylvania; and at the left, at either side of a Rhode Island maple tavern table, are side chairs with recessed curved stretchers. A walnut dresser holds pewter made during the first half of the nineteenth century in the southern part of the United States. Eighteenth-century prints of patriotic subjects line the wall. Near the foot of the stairs is a red-painted music stand.

Imlay Room

An example of American metalwork in the Imlay Room is a three-branch brass candlestick with an adjustable tin shade painted green; the base bears the embossed seal of Baker, Arnold & Co., of Philadelphia. Also displayed here is a pair of spectacles with extension temples; the silver case engraved with an early owner's initials.

William Poyntell operated first a jewelry and stationery store at 21 South Second Street in Philadelphia, and in the 1780's expanded into the manufacturing and importing of paper hangings, advertising wallpapers of "the most modern and tasty patterns, suitable for every part of a house." About 1790 John Imlay, a Philadelphia merchant who had prospered in the West Indies trade, retired to Allentown, New Jersey, and built there a large house in which he used wallpapers purchased in Poyntell's shop. The paper from one of the upstairs rooms is the dominant feature of the Imlay Room at Winterthur, while the paper from another room is in the collection of the Metropolitan Museum of Art, where the original bill from Poyntell, dated April 18, 1794, is also preserved. The mantel, with plaster composition ornament probably made by Robert Wellford, is from the Peter Breen house in Philadelphia; and the fireplace opening is framed with Liverpool tiles decorated with green transfer-printed designs of classical urns. The garniture of Chinese export porcelain complements the gray background and delicate arborescent design of the wallpaper, which is accented by a narrow black border above the chair rail and a wider one beneath the cornice.

In the room are painted chairs and tables from Baltimore, where such furniture is known to have been of rare refinement and style. A pair of open card tables, painted red and highlighted with gilt decoration framing clusters of roses, are here arranged for play with cards and ivory dice cups. Around the table at the left are side chairs also painted red and featuring a back design of crossed bars, accented with gilt ornament. In the corner a semicircular side table, painted black with landscape vignettes within gilt outlines, holds a Philadelphia brass candlestick, a painted watch box, and Chinese porcelain animals. At the left of it is a side chair embellished with musical trophies and other neoclassical elements; a window seat from the same set, with a cushion of striped silk, stands beneath the window shielded by a narrow-slatted green Venetian blind which is contemporary with the wallpaper.

The polescreen, its mahogany shield covered with painted decoration, is of New England origin, as is the maple worktable standing next to an armchair which is yet another example of Baltimore painted furniture. A mechanical bellows is in front of the fireplace; the brass andirons marked *Allison* possibly were made by the Samuel Allison who was listed as a brass founder in the New York *Directory* for 1815. Both the gay spirit of the painted furniture and the delicacy of the wallpaper design is repeated in the pattern of the Bessarabian rug, which has the date *1805* woven into the black background.

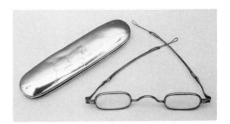

Baltimore Room

The furniture in the elegant little Baltimore Room represents the fine craftsmanship for which that city became known in the years between 1790 and 1820. A colorful background is provided by the blue-and-gray wallpaper, entitled *Vues d'Italie* and showing the Bay of Naples. Printed by Dufour and Leroy in Paris, this set was brought to America by Elisha Dyer, who purchased it on his wedding trip in 1833 with the intention of using it in his country house at Warren, Rhode Island. The dado and the trim of the graceful three-part window, painted a cocoa shade, are from Montmorenci, built at Shocco Springs, North Carolina, in 1822.

The lavish use of inlay by Baltimore cabinetmakers is illustrated by the bellflowers, bowknots, and tassels on the kidney-shaped mahogany card table in front of the window. The shield-back side chairs show molded and petal-inlaid splats and the half-upholstered seat rail often associated with Baltimore. Both the chairs and the card table were included in the exhibition held in 1947 at the Baltimore Museum of Art, which defined the characteristics of Baltimore furniture. Against the wall stands a mixing table, its frame painted black with gilt decoration, and the arrangement on the gray marble top suggests legendary southern hospitality. Shown here are pairs of silver beakers by John Lynch, of Baltimore, and Myer Myers, of New York; a set of six by John B. Akin, of Danville, Kentucky; and single beakers by Samuel Kirk, of Baltimore, and Henry Andrews, who worked in Philadelphia and Boston. Dark-colored blown-glass whiskey bottles, each impressed with the name of the original owner, are flanked by silver candlesticks bearing the mark attributed to John Owen, who worked in Philadelphia from 1804 until 1831. In the center of the table is a silver ewer awarded to Herman Ten Eyck Foster, grandfather of Henry Francis du Pont, for "first premium on farms" in New York State.

On the card table are cut-glass decanters made at the New Geneva Glass Works near Pittsburgh and presented by Albert Gallatin, Secretary of the Treasury under Jefferson, to his friend E.I. du Pont. A glass oil lamp hangs from the ceiling, and an Aubusson-type carpet covers the floor.

Cut-glass decanters made at the Gallatin factory near Pittsburgh and given E.I. du Pont by Albert Gallatin are shown in the Baltimore Room, as is a silver beaker by Samuel Kirk, of Baltimore.

Baltimore Drawing Room

The plan of the Baltimore Drawing Room, placing the chimney breast on the wall at right angles to the window wall, is typical of the front rooms in Baltimore town houses at the turn of the nineteenth century. The mantelpiece here is decorated with plaster composition ornament and contains the central medallion depicting the Battle of Lake Erie, attributed to Robert Wellford's American Manufactory of Composition Ornaments. Details in the plasterwork are similar to those found in Baltimore houses and recall the statement in Wellford's advertisement that "orders from any part of the Continent [would be] punctually attended to, executed with elegance and dispatch."

Light-green walls and ivory-colored woodwork form a background for Baltimore furniture of the Federal period, which is characterized by an elegance achieved with delicately proportioned forms and a lavish use of veneers and exquisitely detailed inlays of satinwood or panels of painted glass. The outstanding piece of furniture shown here is the cylinder-front secretary, made in Baltimore about 1795 and topped by a carved wooden eagle, the American shield emblazoned on its breast. The shelves of its cabinet are filled with Staffordshire silver-resist lusterware, and the American eagle is repeated in the inlay of the cylinder top. The chair at the desk is upholstered half over the seat rail, a common practice in Baltimore. A graceful Baltimore sofa covered with eighteenth-century yellow silk stands beside the fireplace, and next to it a mahogany urn stand holds an English creamware punch pot. In the corners are marble-topped candlestands decorated with eglomisé, or painted glass, panels, one of which portrays the mythological figures of Diana and Endymion taken from a design in Sheraton's *Drawing-Book*. Facing the sofa are Massachusetts upholstered armchairs with concave backs, and on the Maryland drop-leaf table in the foreground is a silver tea set made by Joseph Richardson, Jr., of Philadelphia.

Reflecting the taste of the Federal period are the numerous bibelots in the room. The Argand lamps on the mantel and the candlesticks in the corner have bases of blue-and-white Wedgwood jasper ware. Silk needlework mourning pictures, popular items of sentiment, hang on the walls; and over the fireplace is a water color by Antoine Roux of the American frigate *President* in the harbor at Toulon. Beneath it is a gilt bronze clock commemorating George Washington. Centered above the wool velours carpet, woven in Utrecht, Holland, for the Spanish market, is an English chandelier with dark-green bobêches and pendant. Gray-blue lampas curtains hang at the window.

Above the mantle in the Baltimore Drawing Room is a water color of the U.S. President by the French artist Antoine Roux. Nearby is a transfer-printed English earthenware punch pot.

The Empire Style 1815–1840

About 1800 the classical revival entered a second phase, and the furniture of the Empire and Restoration in France and of the Regency in England followed a more archeological pattern than that inspired by Robert Adam's interpretation of Roman forms. The leading designers at this time were Percier and Fontaine in Paris and Thomas Hope in London, professional architects whose primary concern was the adaptation of classical forms to domestic use, in furniture as well as in architecture. Reflecting the Greek revival in architecture, furniture was based freely upon Greek models, as symbolized by the *klismos* chair, where the single line of the back and seat rail flows into the incurved legs, creating a graceful and "classic" form.

The Empire style, as it has come to be known in this country, dominated American taste between 1815 and 1840. Houses looked like wooden temples; classical figures supported marble mantels; and the architectural scale of furniture in the taste of the French Empire was appropriate to rooms where woodwork followed the classical orders. The buildings designed by such American architects as Benjamin Latrobe and Thomas U. Walter were characterized by a severe and stately classicism. Charles Honoré Lannuier, who came to New York in 1803 and made furniture in "the newest and latest French fashion," was one of the originators of the neo-Greek, or Empire, style; Duncan Phyfe and others followed suit as New York became the center for the production of furniture in this taste.

Winterthur, as originally built for James Antoine Bidermann, reflected the movement. The house was a Regency villa with Doric columns supporting the roof of the entrance porch. Elements of the interior woodwork form the trim of the Empire Hall, South Wing (opposite page). The cylinder-top desk represents a form which developed during the reign of Louis XVI, but its scale is typical of the Empire style. At the left, a gilt mirror with an architectural cornice hangs above a mahogany worktable made by Lannuier for the Van Rensselaer family of Albany. Against the opposite wall are painted and gilded chairs, their backs showing the leaflike anthemion, a device often used in neoclassical ornament.

Dated 1842, the group portrait by Auguste Edouart, a French artist who traveled in this country, records an American interior furnished in the Empire style.

126

Empire Parlor

*Porcelains in the Empire Parlor display portraits of
George Washington. The urn was possibly made at Sèvres;
the pair of pitchers is attributed to the Tucker factory
in Philadelphia.*

Mrs. Frances Trollope, an Englishwoman whose opinion of the United States was often less than favorable, wrote of New York in 1832 that the "dwelling houses of the upper classes are extremely handsome and very richly furnished." Such a comment is applicable to the Empire Parlor, where the woodwork, including the handsome cherry doors, is from the house General Rufus King built in Albany, New York, about 1839. Doorways and window trim formed of pilasters supporting classical entablatures are elements found in such American books as Minard Lafever's *Modern Builder's Guide,* first published in New York in 1833 and widely used in the vicinity of Albany. Against the mauve wall is a mantelpiece of Italian marble from a house on West Sixteenth Street in New York City; its term supports are reminiscent of the engravings of Piranesi, an Italian architect inspired by the ruins of Egypt and Rome.

The architectural flavor of furniture in the Empire style is suggested by the side table next to the fireplace. The front legs have the form of marble columns resting on gilded paw feet. On top of the table are porcelain vases decorated with the portraits of American heroes, while on the shelf beneath are pitchers made at the first successful American porcelain manufactory, operated by William Ellis Tucker in Philadelphia between 1825 and 1838. On the round table in front of the window is a Tucker tea set, white with gold decoration, originally owned by Emma Mathis Haines, of New Jersey. The window is hung with mull curtains embroidered with silver stars; the stencil-decorated worktable at its left was made between 1834 and 1836 by Roswell A. Hubbard, of New York.

At the center of a green-and-gray Aubusson carpet is a pillar-base table, its round composition top embellished with a painting by Lewis Brantz of the capture of the pirate ship *La Gloria* by the packet *Cornwallis*. A side chair illustrating the popular *klismos* form is at the left of the table; its slip seat is covered with silk of the shade usually described as "Empire green." Numerous objects of ormolu ornament the room, and the scene is reflected in pleasant distortion by the convex mirror above the mantel.

Empire Hall

In the Empire Hall are important oil paintings of naval engagements in the War of 1812. Shown on the opposite page are three of a set of six by the French painter, Louis Garneray: The Frolic and the Wasp, The Battle of Lake Erie, *and* The Constitution and the Guerrière. *Their gilt frames are embossed with symbolic military ornaments.*

Patriotism is an underlying theme in the Empire Hall, which suggests in its decoration the nationalistic feelings of Americans in the years following the War of 1812. Pictures of important naval battles in the war, painted by the French artist Louis Garneray, hang on the wall. Their gilt frames are ornamented with patriotic symbols, repeating the spirit of the pier glass which fills the space between the windows. The frame of the mirror is crowned by an eagle carved in high relief beneath a banner inscribed *E Pluribus Unum*. Eagles appear again on the legs of the mahogany and satinwood pier table, thought to have been made in Philadelphia. A French clock commemorating George Washington stands between bronze candelabra on the table top. The desk at the right was once used in the New Hampshire State House at Concord, and on its sloping writing surface is the commission signed by Thomas Jefferson appointing Isaac Hull a captain in the United States Navy. Also on the desk are silver seal boxes, embossed with the American eagle and used to hold the wax seals affixed to official treaties. The eagle motif is repeated in the carved splats of the side chairs attributed to the workshop of Duncan Phyfe, who made similar chairs for Sophia Miles Belden in 1815.

Bright-blue satin with silver-white figures and tape is used for upholstery on the chairs and sofa, in front of which is a rosewood pillar-base table, sometimes described as a "dejuné table" and following a design recorded in 1808 by George Smith in *Designs for Household Furniture*. A French ormolu candlestick is centered on the table; red tole oil lamps are on the stands flanking the sofa.

The arched windows, hung with embroidered mull curtains, and the rest of the trim in the room incorporate elements from Montmorenci, built at Shocco Springs, North Carolina, in 1822. The English rug is contemporary with the woodwork; its pattern is similar to that of the Axminster carpets purchased in 1822 by the great Regency architect, Sir John Soane, for his house in Lincoln's Inn Fields, London.

Empire Bedroom

Reflecting the taste of the 1820's are such objects in the Empire Bedroom as a shell-shaped fitted sewing case (facing page) and a pair of doeskin gloves stamped with the portraits of Washington and Lafayette. A plate from the magazine (right), Meubles et Objets de Goût, suggests the design source of the bed hangings.

The woodwork in the Empire Bedroom, embellished with plaster composition ornament, is from the house on South Tenth Street in Philadelphia built in 1812 by Robert Wellford and later lived in by Peter Breen. Trim from the same house is installed in the McIntire Bedroom (page 88). Here, the chalk-white woodwork is offset by pale-blue walls approximating the color of the Louis XVI figured silk used for the curtains and bed hangings. A French tapestry-weave carpet, with multicolored flowers on an olive-brown field, almost covers the floor.

Alabaster candlesticks and a green silk candle screen grace the marble top of the small stand at the foot of the mahogany sleigh bed, which dates from about 1815 and represents a form often seen in contemporary views of interiors in the Empire taste. The bedcover and the drapery suspended from a mahogany crown are adapted from an illustration of a *Lit Ordinaire* in *Meubles et Objets de Goût,* a magazine of taste and fashion published in Paris by Pierre la Mésangère between 1796 and 1831. The plate referred to here was issued in 1802. The seat of the mahogany side chair in the background is covered with cherry-colored satin appliquéd with red-and-white tape matching that on the bed hangings. Above it is a picture painted in oils and inscribed in the margin: *Sacred to the Memory of Peter Van Vechten and his Child Judith Van Vechten.* The execution of such pictures was a popular feminine pastime in the nineteenth century; theorem painting, another art practiced by young ladies, is illustrated by an octagonal coat of arms hanging above the memorial painting. At the dressing table, which is covered with the same blue silk as the curtains and bed hangings, is a painted chair made in New York by Fredericks and Farrington. The gilt looking glass above the dressing table shows the bulbous turnings characteristic of the later Empire style.

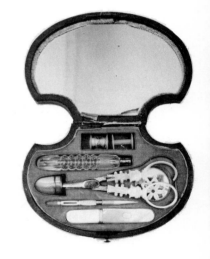

The Empire Bedroom indicates the latest period of American decorative arts displayed in the Winterthur collections; and the emphasis shown here on bold, heavy decoration, the use of elements from various design sources, and the interest in large, massive forms points to the elaborate designs of the Victorian period, when machine production gradually eliminated handcraftsmanship from the decorative arts.

Special Collections

Special Collections

The essence of Winterthur is in the great variety of objects forming this assemblage of American decorative arts which contains the largest and most comprehensive collection of American furniture. Complementing the furniture, however, are many smaller collections, the importance of which is not always recognized, for the manner in which they are displayed emphasizes their contribution to the setting of the entire collection rather than their own merits. In this category are the textiles, which, as window hangings, upholstery, and study pieces, include brocades, damasks, toiles, and chintzes, as well as homespun wools and linens. Important Turkish, Persian, and Chinese rugs, English loomed carpets, and American hooked rugs are on the floors of the period rooms. Paintings, silver, and pewter of American origin can be found throughout the house. As arranged in the rooms, ceramics—delft, stoneware, and Staffordshire pottery—suggest their use in earlier settings.

On the following pages attention is drawn to the special collections. In the case of Chinese export porcelain, which played both economic and aesthetic roles in the life of the early Republic, an area such as the China Shop is devoted to its display. So, too, with the glass collection; the story of the infant glass industry in eighteenth-century America is suggested in the room where it is installed. American pottery, primarily simple pieces for everyday use, represents the skills and taste of the potters working in this country. Tools used to shape American furniture are preserved in the Dominy Woodworking Shop. As shown in the Miniature Stair Hall, even toys are worthy of serious consideration.

Interior and exterior architectural elements provide the framework in which the Winterthur collection is seen; but in some instances architecture, too, is singled out. The Court presents house fronts, and the Shop Lane a row of shops; these, in turn, form the background for other collections. Attention is focused on history in symbolic statues and in rooms devoted to the subcultures that contributed to the making of America. In the Shaker rooms, where the woodwork is from a Shaker building in New Hampshire, the various crafts of this particular religious group are brought together. The Pennsylvania Germans, whose distinctive art forms have persisted in some parts of the country until recent years, are represented by a number of special collections; but these objects are so many and so appealing that a separate section is devoted to them.

Hall of Statues

In the Hall of Statues early-nineteenth-century carved wooden
figures stand in company with Pennsylvania slat-back armchairs.
Companion statues representing Justice and Hope (also on the
opposite page) attributed to John and Simeon Skillin, of Boston,
are at the right. Beyond a carved eagle from Plymouth, Massachusetts, is a female figure with a lyre; and in the far corner the
symbol of American Liberty crowns a bust of George Washington.
The girl holding a dove has a Massachusetts history. Completing
the classical theme is the coachmaker's shop sign showing the
goddess Fortuna in a chariot drawn by leopards.

137

Dominy Woodworking Shop

In the Dominy Shop is a smoothing plane (facing page, above) dated 1765, one of the first used by Nathaniel Dominy IV, and a mahogany table cut and shaped by his son thirty years later.

Tools employed in making furniture such as that in the Winterthur collection, as well as the type of shop in which it could have been produced, are shown in the Dominy Woodworking Shop, which stood on Main Street in East Hampton, Long Island, from the mid-eighteenth century until 1946. Here are more than 800 tools used between 1765 and 1868 by three generations of the Dominy family as they carried on their trades as cabinetmakers and clockmakers, made gunstocks and boats, constructed windmills, surveyed roads, and took part in the life of this rural community near the eastern tip of Long Island. The original shop was added to one end of the family house, a shingled salt-box dwelling built about 1715 by Nathaniel Dominy II, who was born in East Hampton in 1684; a clock shop was added to the other end of the building prior to 1800. Both shops have been reconstructed from architectural drawings and are installed next to one another at Winterthur.

Seen through the great wheel lathe in the foreground are the original Dominy workbenches at either side of the shop. Laid out as if for use are the tools used by Nathaniel Dominy IV (1737–1812), including a smoothing plane dated *1765,* and tools later used by his son Nathaniel V (1770–1852), and his grandson Felix (1800–1868). Among them are an oak miter box with N D scratched on the bottom, a frame saw hanging from the ceiling and used to cut veneer, and a pole lathe operated by foot power at the far end of the room. Against the back wall is a plane rack made by Nathaniel Dominy to hold his molding planes; a block knife for shaping rough wood stands at the far end of the workbench, and on the bench is a powder horn carved by one of the Dominys. Hanging from the rafters at the left are rare documents of the cabinetmaker's craft: templates, or patterns, for the cutting of cabriole legs, cresting rails, and chair slats. In the center of the room is a table cut and shaped by Nathaniel Dominy V about 1796 for the use of his family. The table and a rocking chair made by Dominy for his wife, as well as the tools and family account books, were passed down from one generation of Dominys to the next. The entire collection, including the manuscript accounts covering the period from 1762 until 1829, presents an almost unique record of a family of American craftsmen. Its installation at Winterthur and the story of the artisans it reflects adds a new dimension to the exhibition of American crafts.

China Shop

The China trade, which enriched American merchants and filled many American pantries with porcelain dinner services, is recalled by the China Shop. Chinese export porcelain, made expressly for export to the West and often mistakenly called *Chinese Lowestoft,* lines the shelves of this interior from the Bond Apothecary Shop, built about 1800 in Fredericksburg, Virginia. With the lucrative West Indies trade closed to them after the Revolution, the shipping interests of the new nation turned to the Far East; and when the *Empress of*

China sailed from New York in 1784, she inaugurated a fifty-year trade that brought tea, silks, and chinaware into American ports.

Traditional symbols of the Orient, blue-and-white porcelain pagodas, stand in niches at the rear of the shop. On the counter in front of them is a large monteith decorated with an elaborate coat of arms and probably made for an English family. Flanking it are fruit baskets on stands copying a Meissen model and similar to one brought from China by Samuel Shaw, first American consul at Canton. The earliest pattern here is the *famille rose* at the left. Dating from the mid-eighteenth century, such pieces ornamented with rose-pink flowers often followed European silver forms. The platters and dishes arranged in the next arch exhibit the narrow blue border and central landscape medallion popular in the closing years of the eighteenth century. A porcelain figure of a Chinese woman stands between pierced fruit baskets on the top shelf. Also dating from the late eighteenth century is a dinner set within the arch at the right. Ornamented with a border of grapevines, it bears the gilt cipher of the original owners. White porcelain geese stroll along the top shelf, and at the bottom are soup tureens in the form of geese decorated in natural colors. Patterns of various sorts are seen at the extreme right, among them a small green urn bearing the arms of the archbishop of Oporto, a set of plates with a multicolored pattern of tobacco leaves, and plates colored a solid blue-green framing a coronet within a medallion.

A chandelier with wire arms hangs from the ceiling. The Gothic tracery of the bench beneath it provides a curious complement to the pair of bamboo chairs, made in China in the nineteenth century, but similar to chairs brought to the United States as early as the 1790's. Between them a porcelain dog rests on a stand. The rug is a Shirvan weave.

Indicating the variety of Chinese porcelains made for export, the China Shop includes an eighteenth-century figure of a woman and geese similar to forms sometimes devised as soup tureens.

Pottery Room

Candles in an American tin chandelier and in tin sconces light the Pottery Room, where white plaster walls offset the bright glazes of American pottery which is largely of nineteenth-century date. A flowerpot made in the Shenandoah Valley hangs in the dormer window, which, in design, follows a plate in Owen Biddle's *The Young Carpenter's Assistant, or a System of Architecture Adapted to the Style of Building in the United States*, published in Philadelphia in 1805. The upholstered Windsor chairs, New England in origin, are surviving examples of a type that is mentioned in early newspaper advertisements. They stand on an American striped cotton rug.

Most of the pottery shown in the room is red or yellow earthenware fired with clear or colored glazes. The green-glazed pieces on the hanging shelf are attributed to Rhode Island. Other parts of New England are represented by the lead-glazed and slip-decorated pieces in the scalloped shelves below. In the window sill are stoneware jugs from New York and New England. The double doors from a church near Lancaster, Pennsylvania, reveal the Pottery Alcove, where redware animals of all kinds are displayed in a painted dresser. Some of the slip-ware plates on the shelves here are marked by Willoughby Smith, of Womelsdorf, Pennsylvania, who continued the tradition of the potting craft through the nineteenth century.

Miniature Stair Hall

In a corner of the Miniature Stair Hall is a sideboard made about 1800 in New England of mahogany, with inlaid decoration. It is slightly more than 16 inches high.

Exposed rafters in the sloping ceiling of the Miniature Stair Hall give the room the appearance of an attic; and, with toys, dolls, and miniature furniture of all descriptions, it appears to be an attic that would delight the young and the young at heart. The outsized chandelier, painted yellow with green drip pans, contrasts with the miniature objects, some of which, such as the maple Queen Anne high chest of drawers against the left wall, may not have been made as playthings, but as an apprentice's test of skill or as cabinetmakers' sample pieces.

On the floor at the left is a table set for a card game, lighted by a candle in a miniature hurricane shade. Drawn up to the table are three small rush-seated side chairs and a splint-seated armchair. On the chest behind them, minute silver plates and cups bearing English hallmarks are arranged in front of pewter candlesticks. Two early-nineteenth-century toys, both apparently representing the old woman who lived in a shoe, are on top of the high chest. A "fancy" chair, painted yellow, stands in front of a mahogany New England sideboard decorated with inlay and cross-banded veneer; and beside it is a small William and Mary desk with a sloping lid and ball feet. In the window recess an English delft doll made in a sitting position rests on a rush-seated chair. On the window sill above it are a doll's bed, a miniature high chest, and a table set with miniature dishes of food. A small walnut rocking chair painted red stands beside a half-size ball-foot chest of drawers, probably made in Pennsylvania; and in front of it is a model of an early dentist's chair, upholstered with green silk.

Hooked rugs, fashioned with figures of cats and horses which appeal to children, provide a carpet for two nineteenth-century dolls, one of which is reclining on a "fancy Sheraton" settee, painted black with gilt decoration. Another painted settee, red with gilt squirrels on the cresting rail, guards the top of the stairs.

Glass Collection

Examples of American glass from the Glass Collection make an impression both aesthetic and historical. The effort of the German-born John Frederick Amelung to produce glass in the 1790's is recalled by the covered flip glass (far left) engraved with the name of his friend Charles Ghequiere, and by the deep amethyst sugar bowl made for Catherine Geeting, of Washington County, Maryland. The clear glass sugar bowl (right) of similar form suggests the work of the South Jersey glasshouses. Attributed to Baron Stiegel's factory at Manheim, Pennsylvania, is the amethyst pocket bottle, blown into a mold, as was the brandy decanter which was made about 1820.

Red Lion Inn

Paved with a floor of Belgian blocks from Wilmington, Delaware, and stone slabs from Harper's Ferry, West Virginia, the Court, as it is called, has been described as a setting for architectural fragments and street furniture. By the combination of these architectural elements, street lamps, a wooden pump, and an appealing arrangement of Windsor furniture, it captures the spirit of the eighteenth century that Winterthur purposes to portray. Lining the walls of a large interior space are sections of house fronts reconstructed here with some modifications to give the effect of an urban courtyard or a small village square of the late eighteenth or early nineteenth century. Usually seen in semidarkness with light coming from the windows of the buildings, lanterns, and lamps, and with Windsor chairs and benches disposed in small groups, the atmosphere is that of a summer evening of another age.

Laid in Flemish bond, the red brick wall of the Red Lion Inn is from the tavern and store at Red Lion, Delaware, a crossroads on the colonial route from Annapolis to Philadelphia. It had been built there about 1800 on the site of an earlier building where George Washington is known to have stopped, a fact documented by the entry in his diary for March 1791 that he gave his horses "a bite of Hay at the Red Lyon," on the way from Philadelphia to Mount Vernon. With reeded reveals and square-paneled doors retaining their old gray color, the twin entrances with fanlights are characteristic of Delaware architecture. The narrow windows have paneled shutters on the ground level and louvered blinds on the upper stories. It is traditional in Delaware for the shutters to be painted white and the blinds dark green. A carved figure on horseback, perhaps intended to represent Washington, is attached to the wall.

One inn sign hangs from a bracket at the right, and another is suspended in the frame in front of the building. Emblazoned with the American eagle, the second sign is dated *1815* and announces *T. Archer's Inn*. Beneath it is an early octagonal table painted yellow, green, and red in a manner akin to camouflaging. Assembled in hinged units with removable legs, both table and bench can be placed in a large wooden box for transport. Wooden bowls and plates are arranged on the table top. A New England Windsor armchair stands at the right of the door leading to the Red Lion Entrance Hall.

On the wall of the Red Lion Inn is a carved wooden
man on horseback, perhaps part of a shop sign.
The uniformed rider suggests the popular image of
George Washington.

Connecticut
House

Seen from the door of the Red Lion Inn, the clapboarded façade of the Connecticut House represents eighteenth-century New England architecture. American tin lanterns hang at either side of double doors set within an arched frame typical of early buildings in the Connecticut River Valley. Related to designs in William Salmon's *Palladio Londiniensis* (1734), the doorway was originally part of the Bliss house, built about 1750 in Springfield, Massachusetts. The lamppost in the foreground once stood in Danvers, Massachusetts.

Montmorenci

Stone steps lead to the fanlighted door from Montmorenci, built by William Williams at Shocco Springs, near Warrenton, North Carolina, about 1822. Shown here is the center section of the house front. The delicate cornice derives from a Doric entablature; the graceful three-part window with a scrolled pediment complements the design and reeding of the doorway. Lanterns suspended from scrolled brackets cast shadows on the clapboards. The wooden pump is from the Nathaniel Bowditch house in Salem, Massachusetts.

Shop Lane

Among the English earthenware shown in the Kingston Shop is a platter produced for the American market by William Adams and Sons at Stoke-on-Trent and decorated with a view of Niagara Falls. In the Connecticut Shop window is a copy of The American Instructor, *published in Philadelphia in 1787, and intended to "qualify any Person for Business."*

Like the Court, the Shop Lane is a grouping of architectural elements, but here they are related in being shop fronts assembled to achieve the effect of a street and, as shops, they are adapted to the display of special collections.

At the left, Ionic columns frame the entrance to the Kingston Shop, which is painted gray and is from Rondout, the old section of Kingston, New York, where it was built about 1840. Displayed on shelves behind the arched windows and in the fanlight over the door are examples of colorful Staffordshire pottery, dated between 1820 and 1840, with transfer-printed decoration in shades of pink, green, blue, or purple. Some of the patterns represented show romantic landscapes; others are identifiable views of American cities or natural phenomena and presumably were manufactured for the American market.

A small Windsor settee stands in front of the Connecticut Shop, where bowed windows and a delicately molded doorway, dating from about 1805 and originally from Connecticut, are set against weathered gray clapboards. Within the windows is a collection of late-eighteenth- and early-nineteenth-century books, many of them published in Philadelphia or Wilmington, Delaware.

Across the end of the lane is the China Shop (described in detail on page 140). The dentil cornice, supported by reeded panels and following the line of the curved windows, is from a shop built about 1795 at the corner of South Fairfax and King Streets in Alexandria, Virginia. The double doors are from a contemporary building in Paris, Virginia. Through the windows can be seen a large group of nineteenth-century Chinese export porcelain decorated with an Oriental interpretation of the Signing of the Declaration of Independence.

At the right are the projecting windows of the Baltimore Shop, once at 832 South Hanover Street in Baltimore, and dating from about 1840. Visible in the window is a collection of nineteenth-century American stoneware including jugs, pitchers, and ornamental pieces. Appropriately, two of these are inscribed with the name of the maker, Morgan and Amoss, of Baltimore. A carved wooden shop sign representing a goldsmith's arm and mallet, once gilded, is attached to the wall beside the Baltimore Shop. Stoneware crocks and jugs are mingled with Windsor furniture and simple benches in front of the shops. The floor is paved with old bricks, and a gutter formed of Belgian blocks runs through the middle of the "street".

End Shop

The entrance door of the End Shop comes from Chadd's Ford, Pennsylvania, a village a few miles north of Winterthur; and it is so made that a wooden panel could be inserted within grooves at each side to protect the glass panes. The hanging window, with its wooden shutters that might be bolted in front of the glass at night, is from Middleburg, Virginia, and dates from the early nineteenth century. A bootmaker's sign of wrought iron is above the door; and another shop sign, presumably that of a locksmith, hangs on a corner of the Kingston Shop at the right. Seen through the door is the counter in the interior of the End Shop and on it some of the many objects to be expected in a general store.

Two sturdy wooden stools and a three-legged walnut mortar stand in front of the shop window. On the shelves within are porcelain articles produced in Philadelphia at the factory begun about 1825 by William Ellis Tucker. Using as the basic ingredient the kaolin discovered on a farm in New Castle County, Delaware, Tucker was able to achieve a reasonably pure porcelain, for which he received a premium when the Franklin Institute exhibited "examples of American ingenuity and industry" in 1827. Intending to compete with English and French porcelains, the Tucker factory turned out such forms in the Regency taste as the pitchers, vases, and urns shown here. Many of them were decorated with polychrome floral ornament and gilt borders following designs in pattern books that have descended in the Tucker family. Hoping to expand the operation, Tucker formed a partnership with Judge Joseph Hemphill in 1831; but his death, the failure of the Bank of the United States, and the ensuing depression caused the business to decline. Tucker's younger brother, Thomas, who had decorated much of the porcelain, closed the factory in 1838 and turned to operating a chinaware shop, as his father had before him.

The silver on the shelf above the porcelain represents the work of the Quaker silversmith Jesse S. Zane, who advertised in the *Delaware Gazette* in 1796, and James Musgrave, who was active in Philadelphia between 1795 and 1813. Blown-glass apothecary jars stand on the top shelf. Light from the shop spills onto the brick floor of the Shop Lane, and a candle placed in an eighteenth-century American lantern casts shadows on the brick wall at the left.

The two-handled urn in the window of the End Shop is typical of the porcelain produced at the Philadelphia factory operated by Tucker and Hemphill between 1831 and 1838. Decorated with wreaths of brightly colored flowers and gold banding, its design suggests that of contemporary French porcelains.

End Shop

Shelves from Brown's Apothecary Shop, which was built in 1806 and stood at 30 Fulton Street, in New York City, line one wall of the End Shop. A long grained counter from the store in the Red Lion Inn and a glass-topped case with a "leaning rail" once in a store at Chelsea, Delaware County, Pennsylvania, add to the atmosphere of a general store, the symbolic center of small-town life in nineteenth-century America.

The miscellaneous items to be found in such a shop, as well as several specific collections, are shown here. In the window at the far end of the room is the Tucker porcelain mentioned on the preceding page. On the shelves at the left are pewter dishes, mugs, teapots, and coffeepots made in this country between 1800 and 1840. Next to this group is a display of painted tin household objects, largely from Pennsylvania; and on the shelves beyond is more pewter, including porringers and oil lamps. In the last section of shelves are examples of brass hardware and a number of pewterer's molds, among them a porringer mold probably owned by Simon or Samuel Pennock, of Chester County, Pennsylvania.

The counter top is filled with such homely treasures as the flask in the foreground, which is disguised as a lantern; a carved and painted rooster; and toy soldiers guarding a casket containing a figure perhaps intended to represent a circus performer. Toward the far end of the counter is an aquarium, and beyond it, a bird cage in the form of a miniature church. A crockery dealer's sample plate, scales with a marble base, and a druggist's medicine chest complete the array.

Next to the door a wall clock hangs above a butter churn and a low-backed Pennsylvania Windsor chair. The chandeliers, dating from about 1800 and with painted wood shafts, are of American origin; and on the wall at the right are trammel hooks, used in fireplaces to suspend pots above the fire. The heat of the nineteenth-century cast-iron stove would warm the occupant of the Windsor armchair in front of it.

*The End Shop includes a
sample plate indicating the
different borders available,
a bird cage shaped like a church
(left) and dated 1791, and scales
marked by H. Troemer, of
Philadelphia.*

Shaker Dwelling Room

Called *Shakers* because of the dances that were part of their ceremonies, the United Society of Believers in Christ's Second Appearing was one of the utopian religious groups that flourished in nineteenth-century America. Led by Mother Ann Lee, who considered herself God's daughter, they settled near Watervliet, New York, in 1774, dedicated their "hands to work and hearts to God," and lived celibate lives in communities where all property was held in common. Noted for their integrity and industry, the Shakers conducted mail-order businesses packaging seeds, marketing herb medicines, and making chairs which combined "strength, sprightliness, and modest beauty." The communities were divided into families governed by elders and eldresses in strict accordance with the Millennial Laws.

The Shakers believed that the millennium had come; that by sublimating the body's demands and rejecting wordly pleasures, they achieved a state of happiness symbolic of paradise. The tranquility resulting from these beliefs gave the Shakers a serenity that is reflected in their arts. The stark simplicity of their buildings resembles twentieth-century architecture, as evidenced by the Shaker Dwelling Room, where the woodwork, retaining its original mustard-yellow paint, comes from the large stone dwelling house built about 1840 in the Shaker community at Enfield, New Hampshire.

In the room is furniture from other Shaker villages. Based upon traditional forms, its design has been so refined that its very simplicity and restraint is its characterizing feature, exemplified

A colored lithograph hanging near the Shaker Dwelling Room gives a contemporary impression of the dances that were part of the sect's religious ceremonies. Entitled SHAKERS near LEBANON, State of NEW YORK, it shows at one side a fashionably dressed woman representing the "world's people," who often came to watch.

by the Brethren's rocking chair made about 1830 in New Lebanon, New York, the largest and most important Shaker establishment. Also from New Lebanon are the cast-iron stove and the small bed on wheels near the storage wall, which contains built-in drawers and closets. A long dining table, probably from the community at Hancock, Massachusetts, is at the left; and in the foreground is a rocking chair of striped maple, once used by the eldress of the South family at Watervliet, New York, the Shakers' first settlement. The Millennial Laws prescribed that "floors in dwelling houses, if stained at all, should be of a reddish-yellow." The bare floors here are of that color, matching traces of the original paint.

Shaker Dwelling Room

Mother Ann Lee instructed her followers to "provide places for your things, so that you may know where to find them at any time, day or night." Thus the many drawers and shelves in the Shaker Dwelling Room have special significance. On the shelves are oval boxes made in the Shaker craft shops of thin strips of maple, steamed and wrapped around a mold, the pointed "fingers" fastened with copper rivets. Often painted red or yellow, they were sold in nests of graduated sizes. The large box at the right belonged to Eldress Catherine Allen, of the New Lebanon community.

Shaker Storeroom

The wall of the Shaker Storeroom is the reverse side of that in the Dwelling Room and is so constructed that alternate tiers of drawers or closets open into each room. Probably a storeroom in the building at Enfield, New Hampshire, this small room provides for the display of Shaker crafts. Consistent with Shaker custom, a "tilting" chair hangs from the peg rail; a storage box, stained red, is against the wall; and on the stool under the window are bottles of Shaker herb medicine. The handle of the basket on the floor is initialed *ML* to identify its user. On the rack are textiles of Shaker manufacture, including mauve and blue kerchiefs woven of silk produced at the communities in Kentucky.

Rural Pennsylvania Arts

Encouraged by William Penn, the first German colonists came to Pennsylvania in 1683 and settled at Germantown, near Philadelphia. During the next century thousands more came—refugees from religious oppression and the depredations of war in the Rhine Valley—to take up grants in the fertile land of southeastern Pennsylvania. Benjamin Rush, writing about the German immigrants in 1789, noted that "the principal part of them, were farmers, but there were many mechanics, who brought with them, a knowledge of those arts which are necessary and useful in all countries." Often because of religious beliefs, the Pennsylvania Germans kept to themselves, preserving their language, their religious customs, and their art forms; and thus they have maintained to the present time a more homogeneous culture than most of the national groups that have settled in the United States.

The gray stone wall from the Hehn-Kershner house at Wernersville, Pennsylvania, which lines the Kershner Hall (opposite page), suggests the simple and substantial Pennsylvania German architecture. Generally of stone, but occasionally of half-timber construction, the houses of the Germans followed the traditions of their homeland; outbuildings with red tile roofs similar to those in South Germany are still to be seen in parts of Berks County. At times, neoclassical cornices and doorways were applied to the stone buildings, but most of the German farmers cared little about academic architecture and preferred to build great brick or stone barns.

Substantial, too, was the Pennsylvania German's furniture. Derived from their homeland were the two-door closets called *schranks,* the open dressers for pewter or pottery, and the decorated blanket chests. Ornament, applied or painted, followed traditional patterns, often incorporating such age-old religious symbols as unicorns, tulips, and hearts. The same motifs appear on the smaller objects such as pottery, manuscripts, and cast-iron stoves. Fashioned of local clay and embellished with slip or sgraffito decoration, the pottery often bore dates, signatures, even proverbs. The Fraktur drawings, which take their name from a sixteenth-century type face, continued the tradition of manuscript illumination with colorful baptismal certificates, house blessings, and hymnals. Many of the traditional symbols appear on the cast-iron stoves produced at furnaces in Pennsylvania. The best known of these was the Elizabeth Furnace, operated by Henry William Stiegel, who called himself "Baron," lived in a lavish manner, and also produced in a factory near Manheim glass that ranks among the most appealing of the American decorative arts.

Kershner Kitchen

The stone farmhouse that contained the Kershner Kitchen was built about 1755 on a hillside near Wernersville, in Berks County, Pennsylvania. Originally owned by George Hehn, whose father had received a grant from the Penn proprietors in 1735, the house came into the possession of Conrad Kershner, a farmer and captain in the militia, who lived there until 1803. There is a tradition in the neighborhood that it had been built by two German immigrants, a carpenter and a mason who apparently worked in the manner familiar to them in Germany, for the house was related in plan and appearance to other Pennsylvania houses built by German settlers, particularly Fort Zeller, near Newmanstown, and the Christian Herr house in Lancaster. These early buildings featured a ground plan of two rooms: an entry-kitchen separated from a parlor or bedroom by a massive stone fireplace. The two rooms from the first floor of the Kershner house have been installed at Winterthur in their original relationship.

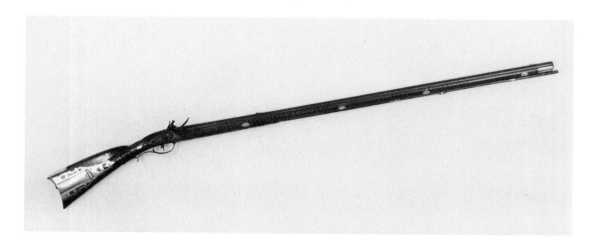

Still showing traces of the whitewash which covered them, the stones of the kitchen fireplace support a twelve-foot lintel of white oak. The floor of the fireplace is laid with the original bricks; and at the right is the corner of the stove opening, through which logs or coals were shoveled into the five-plate stove that warmed the parlor on the other side of the wall. On the lintel hangs a "Kentucky" rifle, its barrel marked by N. Beyer, who worked in Lebanon, Pennsylvania, in the late eighteenth century. As was the custom in Berks County, the logs of the fire are piled upon the hearth without andirons; in front of them are iron pans and a copper teakettle made by Robert Reed, of Lancaster. A toast rack hangs from the lintel at the left, and below it a wafer iron leans against the stone jamb. A painted wall cupboard, each drawer decorated with red tulips, hangs over an early Pennsylvania walnut table. The Windsor side chair is branded by Gilbert Gaw, of Philadelphia, who sold similar chairs to Mount Vernon in 1796.

In the Kershner Kitchen are such items essential to everyday life as a bell-metal posnet (right), a rifle, and a copper kettle, this one made in Lancaster, Pennsylvania, by Robert Reed.

Kershner Parlor

The Kershner Parlor is an extraordinary example of the transfer of European culture to America. Reminiscent of German Renaissance architecture, the molded plaster ceiling has preserved in Pennsylvania ideas the immigrant builders of the Hehn-Kershner house brought with them. On either side of the oak summer beam, baroque cartouches frame medallions which enclose treelike grapevines retaining traces of the original paint, grayed through the years. Twenty-light windows, reconstructed from one remaining original window, are encased in flat, beaded frames painted blue-black to match the first color.

When the room was installed at Winterthur in 1958, its furnishing followed the results of a survey made of household inventories filed in Berks County during the period Conrad Kershner lived in the house. As no rugs or carpets were indicated in the survey, no rug covers the floor here. The cushions on the walnut armchairs, however, reflect numerous references to "check," a frequently used homespun material.

On the walnut sawbuck table are wooden plates, horn cups, pewter tankards made in Pennsylvania, and green glass bottles. Side chairs made in the German style of American woods and often described as "Moravian" chairs, are placed at the table. The armchair at the end is a country version of a Philadelphia Chippendale form. In the corner is a *schrank,* a traditional German form usually included in a bride's dowry. This walnut example is inscribed in wax inlay with the names of Emanuel Herr and his wife and the date *1768.* A box inlaid in a similar manner stands beside a slip-ware flowerpot on the window sill. According to tradition, the leather-covered armchair next to the schrank was owned by the self-styled baron, Henry William Stiegel. On the candlestand beside it is a German pewter candlestick made about 1750. Dated *1774,* the blanket chest, also customary for a bride's dowry, is an unusually early American expression of the form. On top of it, a Bible box, originally owned in Bucks County, holds a German Bible printed in 1748.

Behind the leather-covered armchair stands an inlaid tall clock by Jacob Graff, of Lebanon. The looking glass bears John Elliott's label printed in English and German, indicating that the German-speaking Pennsylvanians constituted a substantial market for Philadelphia craftsmen and merchants.

On the table in the Kershner Parlor is a pewter tankard
with the touch of Simon Edgell, who worked in Philadelphia between 1713 and 1742. Considered to be among
the earliest American pewter tankards, it is engraved with
tulips and foliage and bears the initials A M.

Fraktur Room

The baptismal certificates in the Fraktur Room include one drawn in Berks County in 1771 and ornamented with unusual figures in eighteenth-century dress; another printed in Lancaster County in 1784 by Johann Henrich Otto; and a later example, drawn in 1826, combining an American eagle with traditional decorative motifs.

On the walls of the Fraktur Room are important examples of *Fraktur,* the medieval German art of illuminated writing that lingered in Pennsylvania until the middle of the nineteenth century. Used to ornament baptismal certificates, bookplates, and house blessings, the Fraktur decoration here is characteristic of the lively peasant designs and robust colors enjoyed by the Pennsylvania Germans. The paneling in the room is from the second story of the large stone farmhouse built in 1783 by David Hottenstein near Kutztown, Berks County. The original mottled blue paint on the woodwork, as well as the bold dentiling of the cornice and the architectural treatment of the projecting chimney breast, make this an extraordinary rural room of its period.

Lying on the sawbuck table are illuminated hymnals and school exercise books, their decoration and texts again illustrative of *Fraktur-schriften.* Here also are printed books, one of which is the *Book of Martyrs,* published at the Ephrata Cloisters, near Lancaster, in 1748; another is a copy of Johann Arndt's *Des Hocherleuchteten Theologi* printed in German by Benjamin Franklin. Around the table are walnut wainscot chairs made in Chester County, and in the far corner is a red-and-blue painted desk and bookcase, demonstrating a typical Pennsylvania German combination of a Philadelphia Chippendale form with Continental folk art decoration. To the right of the desk is a painted chest found near Bethlehem, Pennsylvania, ornamented with an unusual Adam and Eve motif also seen in Fraktur pictures. Left of the desk is a chest of the so-called Berks County type, showing painted unicorns and mounted horsemen. Such traditional religious symbols as unicorns suggest, in addition to the Pennsylvania Germans' love of decoration, the religious orientation of their culture.

Slip-ware pottery embellishes the mantelshelf, and earthenware pots on the window sills hold ferns and flowers. The curtains are of eighteenth-century brown-and-white "furniture check," a material often mentioned in Berks County records. American striped rugs of the same date are on the floor. Candles in painted iron sconces and chandeliers light the room.

Pennsylvania Folk Art Room

The product of German-American craftsmen is represented in the Pennsylvania Folk Art Room by a sgraffito plate made by Johannes Neesz, of Montgomery County, in the early nineteenth century; a panel painting of the German Protestant theologian Johann Arndt; and a pewter flask made in Lancaster before 1780 by the German-born Johann Christophe Heyne.

The Pennsylvania Folk Art Room brings together furniture and decorative objects made in Pennsylvania in the eighteenth and nineteenth centuries reflecting both the English and the German cultures that existed there. The white plaster walls, with windows set in deep recesses, give the appearance of a large room in a Pennsylvania farmhouse; the furnishings indicate the various craft traditions drawn upon to complete such rooms.

On the shelves of the pine dresser are earthenware plates and jars with slip and sgraffito decoration. In the style and the method of their decoration, they represent a European craft tradition that persisted in Pennsylvania into the nineteenth century. On the early walnut table in the foreground is pewter made in Lancaster, Pennsylvania, by Johann Christophe Heyne, who settled there about 1757, producing objects in the German manner at first, but gradually adopting forms derived from English usage. The flagon and chalices here were originally intended for church use; the base of the flagon was made in the same type of mold as the plates beside it. At the table is a chair made in Pennsylvania of a design Continental in origin. It contrasts with the red-painted slat-back chair at the left attributed to Maskell Ware, of Roadstown, New Jersey, a region under the cultural influence of Philadelphia. The leather seat of the paneled bench is protected by a cushion covered with homespun linen, and similar material is used for window curtains. Against the far wall is a desk inlaid with a design of vines and berries considered to originate among the English settlers of Chester County, an area which once extended from Philadelphia westward almost to Lancaster. The desk and bookcase inscribed *Jacob Reede,* at the other side of the doorway, is decorated with similar motifs. Its shelves contain additional examples of slip ware.

Suggesting again the religious interests of the Pennsylvania Germans, the painting over the desk represents Johann Arndt, a German Protestant theologian whose writings were widely read in Pennsylvania, some of them published in German by Benjamin Franklin. Beneath the painting are brass oil lamps, and tin sconces flank the door; wrought-iron chandeliers hang from the ceiling. The rug on the floor is woven in multicolored stripes, predominantly brown, pink, and gray.

Kershner Bakehouse

The Kershner Bakehouse preserves the brick oven from the tile-roofed outbuilding (left) on the Hehn-Kershner farm, where bread and pies were baked on certain days and water was heated for the laundry when the oven was not in use. A fire was laid in the oven; and when the bricks had reached the desired temperature, the ashes were raked into a pit beneath the oven floor. An English pewter plate once in the Kershner house is placed among pieces of Pennsylvania pottery on the shelf above the fireplace, and within it an iron pot hangs from a Pennsylvania trammel hook.

Spatterware Hall

Arranged in pine dressers and on a plate rail near the ceiling of Spatterware Hall are numerous patterns of English pottery decorated with colorful sponged backgrounds and freely drawn figures that appealed particularly to the Pennsylvania Germans. At the left is a pink spatterware plate impressed with the mark used between 1825 and 1840 at the factory of William Adams in Staffordshire.

Pennsylvania German Bedroom

The bright colors and bold patterns popular with the Pennsylvania Germans are demonstrated again in the Pennsylvania German Bedroom. Here the dominant architectural feature is the mantel and overmantel from a house built about 1780 near Lancaster, Pennsylvania; the scroll pediment frames a plaster section on which painted jugs hold sprays of foliage. A cast-iron stove of the type developed by Benjamin Franklin is set into the fireplace opening. Andirons cast in the form of soldiers representing Hessians, the German mercenaries who fought with the British in the American Revolution, hold the logs. A copper teakettle rests on a brazier at the side.

Next to the fireplace is a tall clock made in Dauphin County, Pennsylvania, in 1815 for Benjamin and Eva Hammer by John Paul, Jr., a talented craftsman who later applied his genius to designing the famed Horseshoe Curve on the Pennsylvania Railroad. The curly-maple case is inlaid with eagles, the Pennsylvania coat of arms, and the maker's name. A three-legged Windsor table is beside the clock; and, in the foreground, an unusual comb-back Windsor armchair stands next to a chest of drawers painted green and ornamented with yellow birds and conventionalized borders characteristic of the work of Jacob Maser, who practiced his trade in the Mahantongo Valley of Schuylkill County. The chest is dated *1834,* and on top of it is a box decorated with vases of flowers similar to those in the overmantel.

On the floor is an early example of American rugmaking; on a dark-blue background ocher-colored flowers show a pattern similar to those on contemporary bedcovers. At one end is the date *1796.* The Philadelphia barrel-shaped easy chair is covered with an English printed cotton made for the American market about 1830 and featuring framed medallions of the American eagle. Above it hangs a painting, *The Peaceable Kingdom,* by Edward Hicks, the Pennsylvania Quaker who believed that Penn's treaty with the Indians and the peaceful coexistence resulting from it were the fulfillment of Isaiah's prophecy that "the wolf also shall dwell with the lamb..."

In the Pennsylvania German Bedroom a Franklin stove preserves patriotic sentiments of the 1790's with allegorical figures and the inscription Be Liberty Thine, *while Edward Hicks' painting* The Peaceable Kingdom *illustrates the artist's belief that Penn's treaty with the Indians had proved that two peoples might live together peacefully.*

The Dresser Room includes highly decorative household items, among which are a hatbox intended for a tall beaver hat and another one covered with wallpaper depicting New York's city hall, in addition to a colorful hooked rug from New England.

Dresser Room

The Dresser Room derives its name from a group of painted dressers in which are displayed numerous small household objects in use in America in the early nineteenth century. Hatboxes covered with wallpaper sit on top of the dressers, and on the shelves is English pottery made for the American trade. The corner cupboard holds blue-edged ware attributed to the Leeds factory and decorated with representations of the American eagle. In the mottled brown dresser next to it are plates featuring transfer-printed portraits of American military heroes. Some of the plates bear the image of the Marquis de Lafayette and were made to commemorate his return visit to the United States in 1824, when he was hailed throughout the country as "the Nation's Guest." At the right is another Pennsylvania dresser, painted deep red with landscapes on the lower doors. Its shelves are filled with examples of Staffordshire patterns depicting such American scenes as the President's House, Washington; the buildings of Harvard College; and the Catskill Mountain House, a fashionable resort hotel in the 1820's. German toys line the counter in front of the glass doors.

The ten-plate iron stove is cast with delicate neoclassical ornament, as well as a bust portrait of George Washington ringed with stars. It was made at the Catoctin Furnace ten miles from Frederick, Maryland, an area where many German immigrants settled. The Windsor chairs reveal the variations individual craftsmen might make upon the basic method of Windsor construction, which required inserting the legs and spindles into a seat usually shaped of soft pine. The chair with widely raking legs at the right is embellished with scrolls carved on the sides of the hoop back. The armchair shows a turned leg characteristic of Pennsylvania. American hooked rugs are on the floor, and the flax wheel in the center of the room is branded *A·Carr,* perhaps the mark of Alexander Carr, a chairmaker recorded in the 1770's in Trenton, New Jersey, and Wilmington, Delaware. A small tin chandelier hangs from the ceiling, and candles in tin sconces light the wall.

Lebanon Bedroom

The valance on the bed in the Lebanon Bedroom is quilted and appliquéd with a platoon of soldiers clothed in orange breeches and blue tunics.

In the Lebanon Bedroom an eighteenth-century pencil-post bed stands in the center of a space formed by a sloping ceiling that gives the room the intimate quality of an attic bedroom. The bedcover is appliquéd with flowers and borders made of calico and is complemented by the quilted valance decorated with figures of soldiers. Both pieces are of nineteenth-century date. The furniture here is a combination of early and late forms, casually assembled as in a country bedroom. The green-painted armchair beside the bed represents the Pennsylvania slat-back form shown in many variations in the collection. The ball feet and bulbous stretchers suggest a date early in the eighteenth century. Next to the chair is a mid-eighteenth-century candlestand painted to imitate walnut. Characteristic of Pennsylvania is the walnut cradle, its scalloped ends pierced with the popular heart motif. On a rush-seated bench behind the bed, silk bonnets lie on top of a patchwork quilt. An eighteenth-century iron candlestand is beside it, and in the corner is a painted blanket chest made in Lebanon County in 1790 and decorated by Johann Rank. Next to the bed is yet another example of painted furniture—a yellow footstool ornamented with flowers. Hanging from the ceiling is a large tin chandelier painted white; the light of the candles is reflected in the strips of mirrored glass applied to its center section. A rug hooked in a geometrical pattern almost covers the floor.

A variety of forms of decoration are shown here: turned and carved wood, painted surfaces, embroidered textiles. As in many of the rooms at Winterthur, they have been placed together for several reasons: for comparison of forms and techniques, for historical associations, for color, and for appearance. In this way the Winterthur collection symbolizes the skills of American craftsmen in creating the arts of daily life. Assembling the collection and then arranging it for study and enjoyment has been a creative act complementing their efforts.

Index